Motorcycle & Moped Maintenance

CHARTWELL
BOOKS INC.

Published by Chartwell Books Inc.
  A division of Book Sales Inc.
  110 Enterprise Avenue
  Secaucus, New Jersey 07094

© Marshall Cavendish Limited 1978

ISBN   0-89009 – 155 – 2

Printed in the United Kingdom.

INTRODUCTION

Machines are not unlike people. They can generally expect a good life-span barring accidents, and they need feeding, understanding and regular attention to keep them fit for a full and active existence. This book has been prepared to guide the motorcycle or moped owner in mechanical welfare. It explains how and why things go wrong and what action can be taken to cure or avoid them.

It is not a magic mixture to cure all ills. There are hundreds of different machines, thousands of possible ailments. But the book will vastly increase your knowledge in a general way, whether it is to clean a spark plug or take out an engine. And it will certainly make you more sensitive to early symptoms, which means quicker treatment and therefore a saving on more extensive repairs.

As with people, motorcycles will sometimes need specialist help, so when treatment is beyond the scope of do-it-yourself owners, we say so. *Motorcycle and Moped Maintenance* has been prepared by the staff of *Motor Cycle Mechanics*, Britain's top-selling magazine for two-wheel enthusiasts. It is based on their professional experiences and will expand your familiarity with the machine you ride.

CONTENTS

Getting Rolling

Types of machine

Whether you are buying new or secondhand, successful motorcycle or moped maintenance begins with a good machine. Choosing one of the right size and power to fit your needs, or one which has been looked after carefully by its previous owner, will pay dividends later.

Buying a new bike should be easy once you know what you want and how much you can afford, simply by arranging a compromise between the two.

However, getting the best bike for your needs means a lot more than setting up the best financial deal. First, there is the extremely wide range of choice; there are new bikes and used bikes, big bikes and little bikes, high performance bikes and economy bikes, exotic bikes and cut-price bikes – the list goes on and on.

Compared with other forms of transport, any motorcycle over 125cc can be called 'high-performance', so perhaps the best way to categorise machines is in terms of engine size – big bikes and little bikes.

The moped
Starting with the smallest, there are the very basic mopeds, with 50cc engines, as well as a range of step-throughs and small motorcycles going up to 120cc. The 50cc machines – not counting the 'sports' mopeds – are essentially motorised bicycles. They are simple, functional, ultra-reliable and easy to operate, as well as being cheap to buy and run. They usually have one gear with an automatic clutch and a top speed somewhere between 25 to 40 mph. Some of these smaller machines are very cheap to keep on the road and will give more than 100 mpg. As a daily runabout; to get down to the shops (most have a small luggage carrier); or to get to work if it is not more than a few miles, they are ideal.

Their biggest disadvantage is their lack of performance. This can make riding in traffic rather hazardous, as the machine will be continually overtaken by other vehicles and the rider is forced to proceed cautiously. Anyone who buys one as more than a means of basic transport will be sadly disappointed.

The commuter machine
The slightly larger scooterettes and small 'commuter' machines, usually of around 100cc, offer more performance, having gears and a top speed of 50 to 60 mph which at least allows the rider to hold his or her own in town traffic. This kind of machine is a little more expensive to run than a moped, but is still one of the most economic forms of transport. It is also important to remember that this is all it is intended to be. While the machine will obviously cope with more than the daily short journey to work, its scope – in terms of performance, comfort and the ability to carry a passenger – is limited.

It is possible to buy a larger machine in the same price

bracket and several makes are imported from Communist countries which have subsidised prices. These machines are, however, very basic and often do not give much more performance. Their biggest failing is that usually they are not as well finished or as reliable as the Japanese machines.

Moving up into the 125 to 200cc class, the choice is wide with all the big-four Japanese manufacturers and several of the European makers competing with machines suitable for longer distance commuting and short distance touring. Also in this capacity class are the trail bikes. These machines, which are basically a compromise between road and trail bike design, offer the attractive styling of a 'dirt' bike – plenty of ground clearance, upswept exhausts and block-tread tyres – while also being suitable for road use. As with all compromises, however, these machines perform neither role particularly well.

The 250cc class

The 250cc class is worth looking at separately. All of the Japanese manufacturers regard it with some importance, for it is the prestige class in the lightweight group. Again, this group can be broken down into road and off-road bikes but usually in this class it is the genuine article rather than a compromised machine.

Nearly all the larger manufacturers produce machines in this capacity class, with both two-stroke and four-stroke engines. In fact, one of the main choices to be made is between two and four-stroke machines. Two-strokes offer more performance, but with increased fuel consumption. Four-strokes on the other hand offer steady if more leisurely power, but better fuel-economy.

To some extent this choice is being made for you by the manufacturers, as four-stroke models are replacing two-stroke designs in all classes.

As a class, 250cc roadsters have a lot more to offer the serious rider than they are generally given credit for, and they are a lot cheaper to insure and maintain. They also have adequate performance and carrying capacity to deal with sore long distance motorway riding.

Middle-weights

Until recently a middle-weight motorcycle had either a 350cc or 500cc engine. Now, with larger engines of anything up to 1,200cc the term is generally accepted to embrace machines over 250cc and under 650cc – and there is a good selection. The largest choice of bike is to be found in the Japanese range, although there are machines from Germany, Italy, Czechoslovakia, Russia and even India in this class.

In many ways middle-weight bikes, especially the four-strokes, can be considered the ideal all-purpose machine. Light enough for town use, they are fast enough by most people's standards as well as being powerful enough for all but the longest tours. They are also reasonably economical to run and maintain.

Opposite page and top: only 50cc, but the Honda SS50 sports moped has a 5-speed gearbox and a front disc brake.
Centre: Kawasaki KH250, the world's only three-cylinder 250cc machine.
Bottom: a middle range motorcycle, Kawasaki's triple cylinder KH400 is a scaled down superbike.

Superbikes

Known as the superbike class, the over 750cc category is one of the most hotly contested capacity groups. It is the prestige end of the market and the place where every manufacturer has to be represented if he is going to sell smaller capacity machines. Strangely enough it is not a section of the market that the Japanese have completely conquered. While the big Japanese multis easily outsell the European-made twins and triples, Japanese manufacturers have never been able to produce a big bike that would steer or handle as well as European machines. However, this situation is changing rapidly. The new generation of Japanese multis have much-improved handling characteristics.

The superb range of BMW flat twins are probably among the best of the European bikes. These bikes are excellent touring machines and are extremely reliable. The Germans, however, are not without competitors. Ducati, MV, Laverda and Moto-Guzzi keep the Italian flag flying with a range of good performance machines. Also in this class is the overweight Harley-Davidson, offering vee-twin pulling power with very little else!

The problem with assessing bikes in this class, is that 'style' and character have an enormous effect on a buyer's choice. This is another reason why the Japanese have not yet completely conquered this part of the market. For only in the superbike range will image outsell reliability.

Top: One of the quicker production sportsters, Laverda's 1000cc Jota.
Bottom: twin cylinder simplicity from Japan, the Z750 Kawasaki.
Opposite: one of the new generation of Japanese multis, the Suzuki GS550.

Buying secondhand

Secondhand bikes can be bought either privately or from dealers. Both sources have advantages and disadvantages. A private sale may result in a real bargain, but if you make a mistake you will have no 'come-back'. Dealers on the other hand will seldom let a bargain slip by, and will generally over-price their machines, but against this they will usually offer some kind of warranty to cover certain possible after-sale failures.

The best tactic to adopt when buying secondhand is never to accept anything at face value, and that means checking everything very thoroughly. If you are not knowledgeable about the workings of motorcycles and do not feel confident about checking a machine yourself, then take somebody with you who is.

The first rule is not to be rushed into making a decision. Bikes in the secondhand sales area of many showrooms tend to be displayed in long rows which makes it extremely difficult to get round any one machine for a closer look. Obviously, the dealer will pull a bike out of the row for inspection but try to get the machine taken outside the showroom where natural daylight will show up finish defects.

Obvious checks

Check the obvious things first. Tyres, if the tread is down to 2mm (0.8in) or less, will need replacing, and this is not cheap to do especially on a large machine. The same goes for the final drive chain which can quickly be checked for wear by taking up the slack with a finger on the bottom run of the chain and then, with the other hand, pulling on a link on the rear sprocket. If the chain has stretched there will be play on the sprocket links.

Correct spoke tension can easily be checked by running a pencil around the wheels. If all the spokes are equally tensioned and undamaged they will ring with the same note. Cast wheels need very close inspection for fractures because they cannot be repaired and are very expensive to replace.

Frame checks

After the superficial checks, next it is vital to check for any possible frame damage. First look for bent or cracked tubes and fractured welds. Then put the bike onto its centre stand and check alignment by sighting along the wheels. If the wheels fail to align and the spindle adjusters are on the same marks the reason could be a bent frame. Check the front forks for any possible damage and make sure the chrome on the staunchions is not pitted or rusted, as this will destroy the fork-leg oil seals. Try the damping action of the forks by pushing the bike forward with the front brake on. The forks should depress smoothly and there should be no signs of oil seepage. They should also return fully, once released. Putting the bike back on its centre stand, turn the handlebars from lock to lock. If any roughness can be felt, or the bars do not turn easily all the way through their movement, the steering head bearings either need replacement or adjustment.

A frequently neglected, but vital maintenance job is the lubrication of the rear swinging arm bearing. Wear here can be detected while the bike is still on its centre stand by taking hold of the swinging arm in one hand and the sub-frame in the other and pushing and pulling sideways on the swinging arm. There should be no sideways movement at all. If there is you must get the dealer to put it right. Replacement of a swinging arm bush can be very difficult without the proper

tools. While you are around the back end of the bike examine the rear dampers for signs of leaking fluid.

Brake checks
On earlier models with drum brakes, a rough idea on the condition of linings can be gained by looking at the angle of the cam arm. The cam should be at right angles to the brake rod or cable. On later models, lining wear indicators are fitted as standard. On bikes with disc brakes the discs should be examined for deep score marks. Badly scored discs will greatly increase pad wear and reduce braking efficiency. On chromium-plated discs the condition of the plating should be closely inspected. If the plating has broken up or is heavily corroded it will tear the brake pads to bits very quickly. Even more important than the condition of the discs and pads are the hydraulics. The complete systems for front and rear brakes should be checked, not only for leaks but also for chafed and badly-positioned fluid lines. If there is any doubt at all about the hydraulics they can be tested by putting the brakes on very hard and keeping them on. Neither the foot lever for the back brake, nor the hand lever for the front brake, should move. If either does it means that somewhere fluid is escaping.

Electrical checks
Unless you know what you are looking for, electrical faults on modern machines can be extremely hard to trace – so lights, horn and indicators should all be tested to make sure they work properly. Note the general condition of wiring and take a close look at the battery to make sure that the terminal posts are not corroded or loose. On electric-start models test that the starter has power enough to turn the motor over and does not make any undue noise.

Engine checks
It is at this stage that the motor can be examined. But before starting it up, give it a close look over. Two things that you should look for are signs of oil leaks and the over-use of gasket jointing compound. The latter could indicate that the previous owner had had the engine apart and that could be expensive for you!

Next, have the bike started. Note how easily it starts. Two-strokes usually smoke a little, but if the exhausts of a four-stroke smoke heavily after the engine has warmed up then suspect either worn valves or guides, or worn piston rings or bores. While the motor is still relatively cold, piston slap can easily be identified and this is another sign of serious engine wear. As the engine warms up and the oil thins out, small-end noise will reveal itself as will big-end and main bearing noises. Big-end noise shows up most readily when the engine is under

Top: for those who want something really different – the rotary engined DKW.
Centre: noted for superb roadholding is Ducati's 860 GTS vee-twin.
Bottom: two big bikes from Italy that put Moto Guzzi on the motor cycling map are the T3 tourer (left) and Le Mans – definitely for the experienced rider.

load and worn main bearings whine or rumble and are usually the cause of heavy vibration. All these noises, however, are not easy to distinguish, hence the need to have someone experienced with you before buying a secondhand machine.

One of the most exotic machines yet produced is this in-line, six-cylinder monster from Benelli, 750cc of pure luxury and power. It is not exactly a common sight on world routes but definitely something for the enthusiast to covet.

Test drive

The next step is to ask for a ride on the bike. Almost certainly the dealer will refuse but most should be able to arrange a ride on the pillion. There is no point in buying a secondhand bike without having ridden it; for many possible faults will not show themselves until the bike is on the road.

Out on the road the things to listen for are clean carburation through the gears and the engine note – smoothness during acceleration is the key here. Again, watch for excessive smoke; on two-strokes it indicates incorrectly-set automatic lubrication; on four-strokes it usually means that the engine is badly worn. Listen also for transmission whine and for 'clunking' when the gears are changed. Check that the gears stay in engagement when the engine is pulling under load. Make a

note also of how the motor idles once hot. On two-strokes this is particularly important, because stroker engines with worn crankcase seals will race.

By this stage you should have a pretty clear idea of what the bike is worth to you, and all that remains is to negotiate a compromise between your price and that on the price tag. How easy that is likely to prove depends on several factors and they are worth bearing in mind. For instance, it is unlikely that a dealer will drop his asking price by very much if the machine is in ready demand. It is also worth remembering that the spring and summer months are peak selling times for motorcycles and prices tend to be higher than during the winter which is by far the best time to go looking for a bargain.

Tools for the job

These days most machines are provided with a tool kit adequate for minor repairs and adjustment. If you want to do any more than this, however, you will soon find that you need a better and more varied selection. The next step then is to build up a tool kit of your own. As this can be expensive careful consideration should be given to choosing which tools to buy, and to their quality.

Usually, the more you pay for tools, the better quality they will be. However 'quality' in this sense is relative to how the tools will stand up to use, as well as to how well they are made.

So if your aim is simply to put the odd fault right and do basic maintenance then medium-priced tools will be quite adequate.

Those tools which you consider essential will again depend on the particular jobs you plan to do. It is usually best though, to build up a basic set first. This will include a variety of spanners – open-ended, ring and socket types; several screwdrivers both for slot and cross-head screws, an impact screwdriver, pliers, a hammer, feeler gauges and a variety of extras such as a chain-splitter, a torque wrench and a circuit tester. For touring carry a few spare components.

Spanners [wrenches]

Before buying a spanner [wrench] of any type, you must first establish what type of nuts and bolts are used on your machine. The majority of bikes on the road today use metric-sized nuts, but some American and British machines have A/F (American Fine, Across the Flats) sizes. These sizes are not interchangeable so be sure to buy the right type of spanners [wrenches] for your machine.

Although it might seem wasteful the first spanners [wrenches] to buy are replacements for those sizes contained in the toolkit. This will allow you to generally use better-quality tools, as those provided are usually of poor quality, as well as giving you two of each of the most useful sizes. This is often essential in cases when undoing a nut means holding on the bolt on the other end at the same time.

While open-ended spanners [wrenches] have the greatest general applicability, where possible it is best to use ring spanners [wrenches] or sockets. For these give a better grip on the nut and offer less chance of damaging the nut or yourself. Thus the most commonly used spanners should also be duplicated in ring or socket form too.

Adjustable wrenches are also useful, as there will always be one nut on the bike that none of your spanners will fit. These, however, should only be used as a last resort, because as they are not a precise size they can round-off a nut head quite easily. For this reason it is well worth buying the best you can afford, as the dearer ones usually offer a greater degree of adjustment.

Once you have a complete set of spanners, the next addition you should make to this set is a torque wrench. For while these are invariably expensive they are essential if you intend to do any serious work on the engine. Torque wrenches measure the force applied to a nut as it is being tightened up. This allows for components such as the cylinder head to be

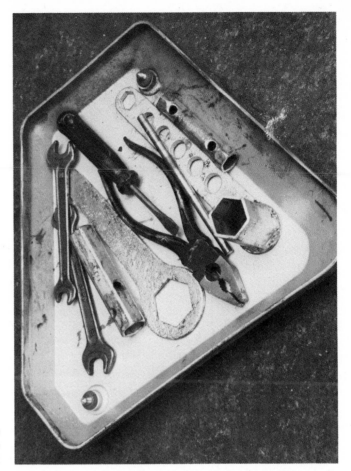

The tool kit supplied with the bike is a start, but quality is usually poor.

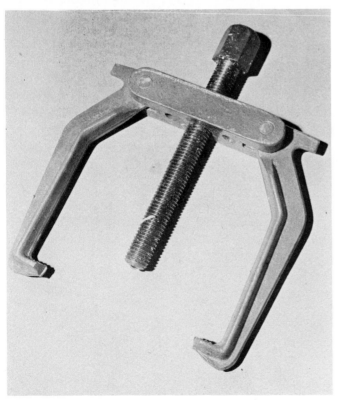

A simple puller can often be substituted for the factory version on sprockets etc.

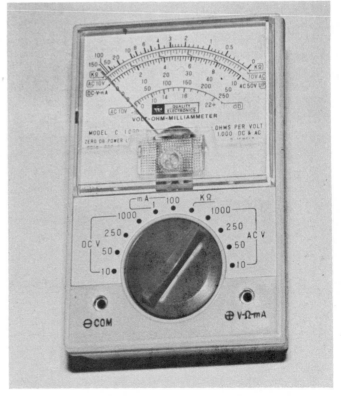

Useful equipment on the electrical side is a voltmeter for trouble tracing.

13

tightened down evenly and to a correct pressure. The bike's handbook should contain all the vital torque settings, and these must be followed.

A point to consider when buying a torque wrench, is that if you already have a socket set buy a torque wrench with the same size drive.

Screwdrivers

You should have at least six screwdrivers in your tool kit. Three should be of the flat-blade type and three cross-blades. Buy the best that you can afford – especially the cross-blade ones. For the cheap screws fitted to many machines today are easily damaged by an ill-fitting screwdriver.

As well as the ordinary screwdrivers an impact screwdriver is almost an essential too. This is because many of the screws used on Japanese machines, for example, are machine tightened. Without an impact driver the screw head will often tear before it will undo.

Other tools

An essential item in your tool kit is a set of feeler gauges. As with the spanners [wrenches], these are made in both metric and Imperial sizes, so check your bike handbook before buying a set.

Other useful tools, which you may have already, include pliers and a hammer. A ball-pein hammer is best, although it should never be used directly, but with cloth or a piece of wood between it and the work.

With the trend today for drive chains to be made in one piece, a chain-splitter is a cheap and very useful tool, and will enable links to be quickly and easily removed.

On the electrical side, a voltmeter or an ohm-meter can both be useful, but to begin with a simple circuit tester comprising of a bulb and two leads is often all you will need.

To do the timing a strobe light will be needed and these can be bought quite cheaply.

More complex tools, such as dial gauges and vacuum gauges, are perhaps best hired, as in relation to their frequency of use they are quite expensive.

Many of the 'special' tools specific to one machine can often be hired too, and this is the best course unless you plan to keep one bike for a long period of time.

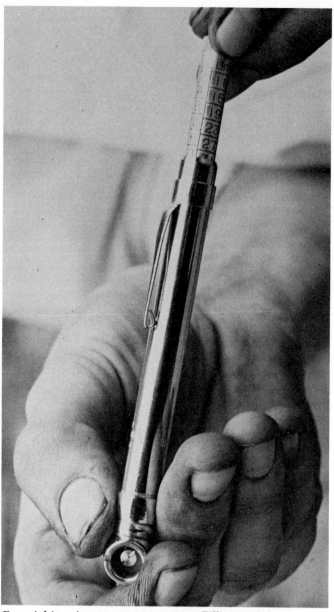

Essential item is a tyre pressure gauge. Filling station ones are often inaccurate.

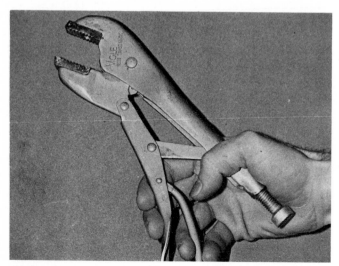

Mole grips serve as a portable vice or third hand in awkward situations.

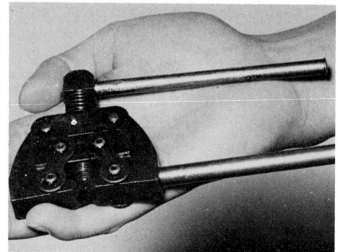

With more endless chains being used, a chain splitter becomes important equipment.

Preventative Maintenance

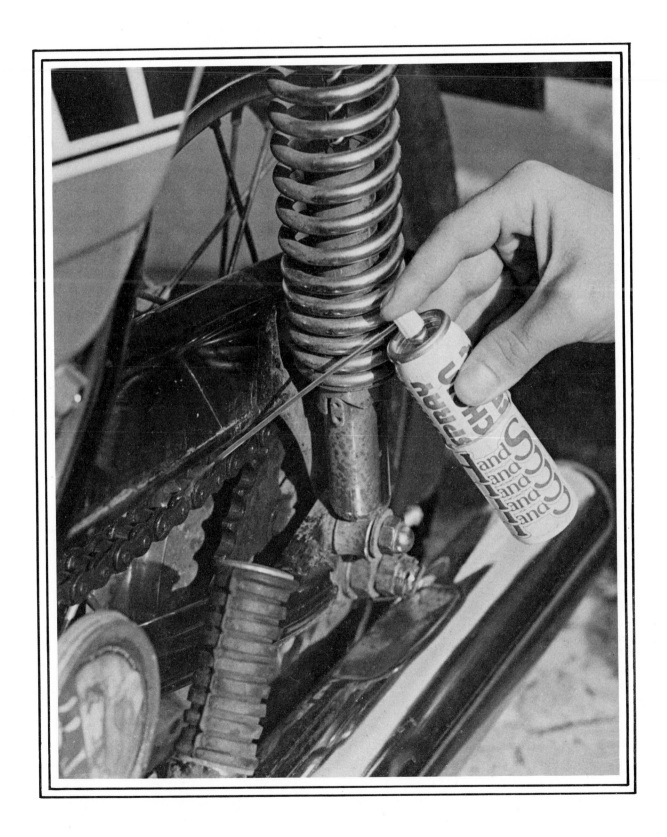

Winning on points

The majority of bikes, particularly the small, high performance ones, are very sensitive with regard to ignition timing. It only needs to be slightly out and the performance begins to drop off. Go a stage further and the results are like running on the wrong grade of spark plug; the plug begins to foul or get burnt away, and there may even be damage to the piston crown.

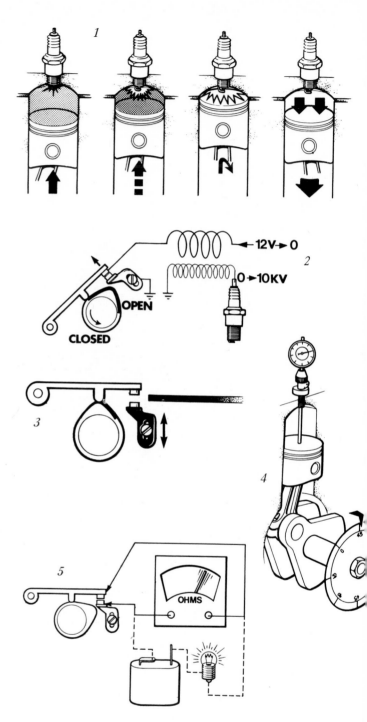

Fig. 1. Why timing advance is necessary. 'Advance' simply means that the spark occurs before the piston reaches the top of its stroke, measured as piston movement, or in degrees of crankshaft rotation. As the piston is rushing up the cylinder, compressing the fuel, the points open and trigger the spark. The mixture begins to burn as the piston gets near to top dead centre and the pressure of the hot gases increases tremendously. Combustion is completed and pressure reaching a maximum just as the piston gets to the top of its stroke, so the full pressure force can be exerted on the piston to give the downward power stroke. The amount of 'advance' depends upon the time taken between the spark at the plug and total combustion of the fuel – in other words on how quickly the fuel can be made to burn, plus the 'rise time'. The latter is how long it takes the current in the coil to collapse and induce the high voltage in the secondary coil winding. The drawings are exaggerated, in practice the timing is advanced by something like 30° at the crank, and the piston is between 2 to 5mm (.008 to .020 in.) before TDC. The actual time taken for this sequence is about 1 to 5 thousandths of a second.

Fig. 2. How the spark is generated. In the orthodox contact breaker and coil set-up, the contact breaker is no more than a switch, opened by a cam which is turned by the engine. The cam is shaped so that having opened the points, they remain open for a specific length of time (called the open 'dwell') and then close. While closed, they complete a circuit from the battery (or generator) through the primary winding of the coil. When they open this circuit is broken and the collapsing current induces a high voltage (10,000 volts or more) in the secondary winding of the coil, which is connected to the spark plug. The closed dwell of the cam has to be long enough to allow the current in the primary winding to build up to full strength again.

Fig. 3. The dwell of the cam controls the amount of time available for the primary current to build up and can be measured with a dwell meter. The usual method, though, is to measure the points gap. When the cam has opened the points to the maximum, the gap is measured by sliding a feeler gauge between the points. It can be adjusted by slackening the screw which clamps the fixed point, moving the point and re-tightening the screw. When the gap is set at the recommended figure – usually .3 to .4mm (.012 to .016in) – the dwell will be correct.

Fig. 4. Timing is set by turning the engine to the position where ignition should happen and then adjusting the contact breaker so that the points are just opening. The position of the piston can be measured using a dial gauge screwed into an adaptor in the plug hole (which must be parallel to the cylinder) and measuring the distance of the piston before

TDC. Or a degree disc can be fixed to the crankshaft and after finding TDC the engine turned back the specified number of degrees. If there is any backlash in the drive to the contact breaker cam, the motor should be turned back more than the specified amount then turned forward to the timing point.

Fig. 5. When the engine is in the correct position the whole contact breaker backplate is turned so that the cam is just opening the points. A piece of thin paper held between the points will just be released when the points are in this position. Alternatively, the switching function of the points can be used

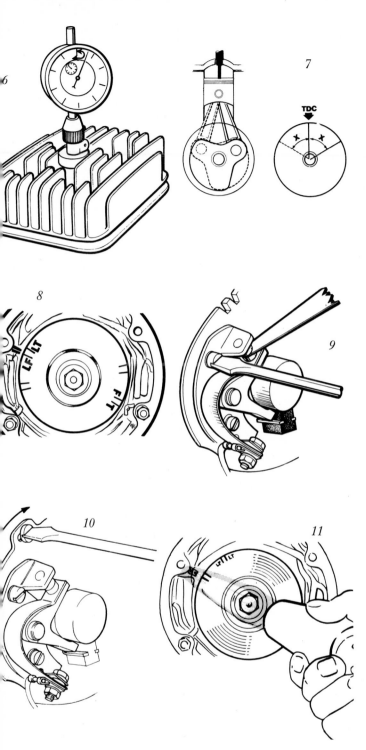

the needle will move around the dial, stop, and start to go back as the piston reaches TDC. The scale should be set to read zero at this point.

Fig. 7. An alternative method is to make a stop from an old spark plug which will bear on the piston about three-quarters of the way up the bore. With a degree disc mounted on the crank, turn the engine until it meets the stop and note the reading of the pointer on the disc. Turn the motor back until it comes up to the stop again and get another reading. The dead centre positions will be mid-way between the two. The engine should be turned to TDC and the pointer set to read zero on the degree disc. Then all other measurements can be taken from this. It is worth taking time to do this accurately as everything else hinges on it. Trying to judge the position by watching the piston is not close enough, because at TDC the piston only moves a few thousandths of an inch for several degrees at the crank.

Fig. 8. Many engines have TDC and timing marks on the alternator rotor or the contact breaker cam drive. Letters L or R or a number usually refer to the cylinder being timed, the T being TDC and the F the static ignition point. The other marks are the limits of the fully advanced timing, for use with a stroboscope. As an example, the marks on the rotor in the drawing are set for the static or retarded timing point on the left-hand cylinder. This is where the timing would be set if it were done with the engine not running, or where a strobe light would 'freeze' the marks at idle.

Fig. 9. To set the contact points, turn the engine until the cam is at maximum lift, slacken the fixed point, slide the appropriate feeler between the points and tighten up so that the points are just gripping the feeler. Check first that the points are clean and are mating squarely. If they are out of line or badly pitted they should be replaced, although slight damage can be cleaned up with emery paper. After adjusting, turn the engine over and re-check the gap, to ensure that the feeler gauge was not lifting the pivoted point.

Fig. 10. Adjust the timing by setting the piston at the right position, then slacken the screws holding the contact breaker backplate. Turn the plate until the cam is just bearing on the heel of the contact breaker and making the points open. Tighten the screws to clamp the backplate. This static timing is done with the ignition fully retarded; with auto advance mechanisms the cam is turned in the direction of rotation by the action of bob-weights. As the engine speeds up centrifugal force on the weights forces them outwards, turning the cam and advancing the timing. The weights are returned by springs as the engine slows down.

Fig. 11. Check the action of the advance mechanism by twisting the cam. It should move freely and return immediately to the original position when you let go of it. A stroboscope connected to the HT leads will show where the spark fires while the engine is running. At idle the timing marks should align with the static mark, and as the engine speeds up the mark should progressively advance until at 2000 rpm or so the 'fully advanced' marks line up. If the timing does not move the right amount, the bob-weight mechanism is sticking or the springs may have weakened. The contact breaker plate will usually have to be removed so that the auto-advance can be overhauled.

by connecting them to an ohm-meter or a light bulb and battery. When the points are closed the light will be on and the ohm-meter should read zero. As they open, the light will flicker out or the meter needle move across to the infinity, or open-circuit end of the scale.

Fig. 6. Finding TDC and setting the piston position is easiest with a dial [depth] gauge, although if the plug hole is off-set the head will have to be removed and the gauge clamped to the barrel. If the head is removed from a two-stroke the barrel should be bolted down otherwise crankcase compression will lift it and break the crankcase seal. When the engine is turned

Cam chains

In recent years the pushrod system of valve operation has largely been superceded by the use of overhead camshafts. The latter is a system which absorbs very little energy, puts the minimum of stress on the working parts and is inherently reliable.

Being a chain-driven system, however, this chain needs some periodic maintenance – particularly to keep it at the correct tension. A well looked-after chain should last over 10,000 miles.

Suzuki

Suzuki's first four-stroke overhead-cam models feature an automatic cam chain adjuster and this needs no maintenance.

A long slipper-tensioner comprising a steel blade with synthetic rubber facings is pressed on to the rear run of the chain by a sprung push-rod. The other end of this push rod is wedge shaped and another rod, at right angles to the push rod, bears against the wedge to stop it slipping back. This locking rod, or adjuster rod, is kept pressed against the wedge by a spring which turns it clockwise against a cam face and the screw action winds it in. This results in the push rod spring pushing the tensioner to take up any slack in the chain, and the adjuster rod dropping in behind the wedge to stop it moving back again.

The knurled disc on the outside of the adjuster body should only be used to check that the adjuster is working properly. This can be done by turning the knurled disc anti-clockwise about half a turn and holding it there while you turn the engine backwards. Release the adjuster and watch it as you turn the engine forward again. It should click back to its original position. This shows that when the chain slackens as you rotate the motor forwards, the tensioner, push rod and locking rod all move in to take up the slack.

Yamaha

Yamaha employ both automatic and manual means of cam chain adjustment. As on the Suzukis, the automatic-adjusters need no maintenance and if they fail it is a job for your dealer.

For the manual adjusting systems the tensioner apparatus is located at the rear of the cylinder and the adjustment is simple. Remove the cap that covers the plunger and spring, then locate the pinch bolt which is on the side of the adjuster casting and slacken it and its locknut off. Next turn the engine over slowly two or three times and watch the end of the plunger as it moves in and out of its body. When it reaches its furthest-in point, stop – do not turn the engine backwards – and tighten up the bolt and locknut. Do not overtighten the pinch bolt or you will snap it or damage the plunger. All that remains then is to replace the cap. Adjustments should be made every 2000 miles and cam chains are recommended to be replaced at around the 12,000 mile mark.

Honda

As Honda have such a large range of OHC machines, with a variety of different methods for adjusting the cam chain, only those on recent twins and four-cylinders are given here.

The method on several of the smaller twins is to line up the 'T' mark on the generator rotor with the fixed index mark; undo locknut and tensioner bolt to let the sprung plunger take up the slack in the chain, then retighten the bolt and locknut.

The larger models are more complex, however. Some of the

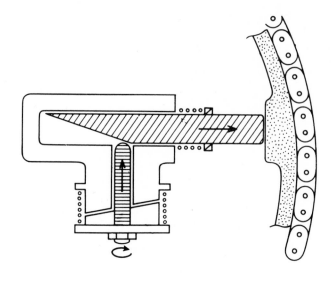

Automatic cam chain tensioner on Suzuki GS750 and GS400 twin overhead cam models.

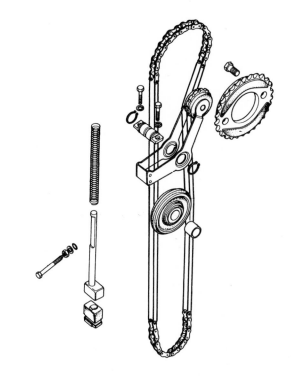

On the six-speed CB250 Honda cam chain adjustment is done manually.

five-speed twins had automatic cam chain tensioners operated by the hydraulic pressure of the oil feed, and these require no servicing other than checking that there are no leaks in the oil system and that it is full.

The later six-speed twins have a manually adjusted cam chain tensioner located underneath the starter motor, and the locknut and pinch bolt are slackened off and retightened when all four valves are closed completely and the tappets are free. This position occurs at 90° after top dead centre on the compression stroke of the left hand cylinder. Set this by rotating the engine anti-clockwise until the index mark on the stator is at 90° after top dead centre. If the tappets are not free, rotate the motor 360° and try again. With the crankshaft now in the correct position the pinch bolt can be backed off to let the sprung plunger take up the chain slack, then re-tighten and lock.

There are two ways of adjusting the cam chain on the four-cylinder models. One model requires that you start the engine and set the idle to 1200 rpm before loosening the locknut and tensioner pinch bolt right off and then retightening. Other four-cylinder engines are adjusted with the motor dead, and the only variations are in the locknut design.

First remove the tappet covers for No. 1 cylinder, remove the contact-breaker cover and align the $\frac{1}{4}$ 'T' mark with the fixed index point, then check that the valves on No. 1 cylinder are free. If not, rotate engine through 360° so that they are. Now rotate the crank clockwise until the spring peg on the advancer assembly ($\frac{1}{4}$) is just to the right of a line drawn vertically through the fixed timing mark. This is at 15° after top dead centre. Loosen the locknut for correct tension, and re-tighten. Do not push in the plunger or you will cause damage. Then refit the parts removed.

Kawasaki

All Kawasaki four-strokes have manual cam chain adjustment. The mode of adjustment is basically the same for each, but differs slightly in the location of the adjusters which can be at the front of the cylinder or at the rear. Some models use slipper tensioners while others can have slippers and rollers or just rollers.

The basic method is to remove the tensioner cap and 'O' ring (rear or front of cylinder) and remove the generator cover to get at the crankshaft-end nut. With a spanner [wrench] on this nut turn the crankshaft anti-clockwise and watch the push rod in the centre of the adjuster body. It will move in and out as the engine is turned and you should stop turning the engine when the adjuster is furthest in. Do not turn the motor clockwise even a fraction to reach this point, as the chain tension will be completely altered. If you go past the furthest-in point, go right round again until you come up to the chain's slackest point. Having got the adjuster plunger in its furthest-in position, loosen the adjuster locknut and turn the plunger guide until the end of the guide and the plunger are absolutely flush with each other. Do not go any further. Then tighten the locknut, refit the cap and 'O' ring and the generator cover.

A possible variation to this method on some models is that to turn the crank the contract breaker cover, rather than the generator cover, has to be removed.

All four-cylinder Kawasakis have their cam chains adjusted in the same way, except that the torque settings for the adjuster pinch bolts are different.

First remove the contact breaker cover and, with a spanner on the crankshaft end nut, turn the crank clockwise two turns and then set the flywheel timing marks so that two of the

pistons are at top dead centre. This will be when the $\frac{1}{4}$ or the $\frac{2}{3}$ marks line up with the 'T' mark on the casing. Then undo the chain tensioner pinch bolt locknut and the bolt and make sure they are undone several turns. The spring on the plunger will push it in and take up the slack in the chain. All you have to do is retighten the pinch bolt to the correct torque setting. The locknut should then be tightened down to stop the pinch bolt coming undone.

Again the general rules apply. Never turn the crank in the opposite direction to that specified when setting the cam tension and never overtighten the adjuster pinch bolt.

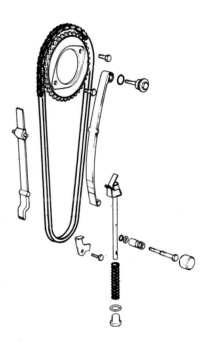

Simple slipper tensioner on the single-cylinder XL250 Honda.

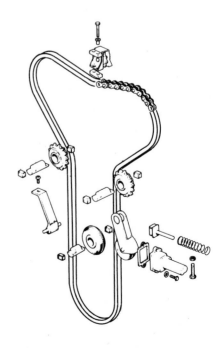

On the Kawasaki double overhead camshaft fours adjustment is from the engine front.

Oils

Motor oil has the basic function of reducing friction, and hence wear, in an engine. It has however, a much more complex role than this, performing many other functions. These include keeping the engine free from dirt and other deposits, aiding engine cooling, and assisting cold starting.

In order to carry out these various functions most oils are full of a variety of special additives.

Wear reduction

The most important and obvious function of the oil is to lubricate, and hence reduce engine wear. This involves acting as a barrier in all the areas where there would otherwise be metal to metal contact.

The main problem in maintaining this barrier is that the engine operates under conditions of very high temperature and pressure against which the oil has to work.

To combat these conditions anti-wear compounds such as phosphorous and fatty substances are added to the oil. Under high temperatures and pressures these additives form a coating over the bearing surfaces and hence continually inhibit wear.

Cleaning action

The by-products of combustion which includes a litre of water for every litre of fuel used, combined with all the dust and dirt which pass through the air filter, pose a serious hazard to an engine – the harder particles such as carbon deposits aid engine wear, while the water and resultant sludge inhibit the action of the oil.

Good quality oils thus have several additives to cope with all this internal 'pollution'. These principally include detergent compounds, which break up the grouping tendencies of some of the combustion by-products, reducing their tendency to form a harmful sludge. This action also results in keeping the piston rings clean and more efficient in operation. This in turn results in less oil entering the combustion chamber and being burnt into harmful carbon deposits. Modern oils also burn more cleanly than the older ones, so few deposits are left anyway.

Cooling action

Combustion chamber temperatures can exceed 1000°C and, while the engine is largely cooled by either its water or air cooling system, the oil also plays an important part.

In many areas – such as where it lubricates the crank bearings – its flow is continued and thus it has the facility to disperse any heat it picks up as it passes through hot bearings. Thus the oil has to be very mobile and have no tendency to cloy or else its role as a dissipater of heat would be lost.

Easy engine start

When an engine is started up, especially when cold, an additional loading is put upon it. This load can be greatly increased or reduced by the viscosity – thickness – of the oil.

Obviously the thinner the oil the easier starting will be. Yet oils thicken at cold temperatures and thin as they heat up. Thus an oil thin enough for easy cold starting may become too thin to be effective once the engine heats up. Multi-grade oils avoid this problem by having an additive called the viscosity index improver. The most commonly used oil is the multi-grade SAE (Society of Automotive Engineers) 20W/50.

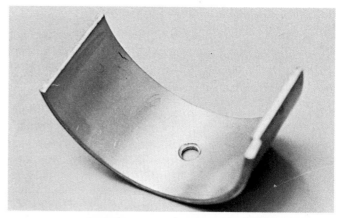

Typical scoring and scuffing on a piston skirt. Result is heavy oil consumption.

New shell bearings (centre) should be well oiled on assembly. Compare it with the scored and pitted one below. The broken surface upsets lubrication.

The numbers refer to the oil's viscosity at two standard temperatures (—18°C and 99°C). Multi-grades behave like a mixture of single grades – a 20W/50 for example will act like a thin 20W grade when it comes to cold starting but like a heavy 50W once hot. This range allows one oil to be used all the year round in all but those areas where temperatures are extreme.

While most machines will accept a multi-grade, such as a 20W/50 or 20W/40, some do run better on a heavier oil such as a single grade 40W. Old under-square or high performance machines, which continually run hot, usually need an oil such as this.

Two-stroke oil

Two-stroke machines run on what is called a total loss system i.e. where oil is used rather than circulated. These engines burn off the oil during combustion and thus require a clear burning oil to at least delay the periods between the essential periodic de-coke.

Because of the way the oil is used single grade rather than multi-grade oils are preferred for these machines – usually of around a 30W.

Additives

Apart from the additives which come as an integral part of nearly all today's high quality oils, others are sold for separate addition. Their effects, however, are likely to be minimal, due to the fact that the original oil is already full of most of the essential 'additional' compounds. Also, for the extra expense over the long term, an oil change would be a better alternative.

Protecting your engine (four-strokes)

However complex the oils are and however efficiently they do the job of reducing engine wear, their effectiveness is reduced over time. No oil can cope indefinitely with all the by-products of combustion, engine swarf, and the dust that comes through the air filter. Thus it is essential that the oil is changed regularly – as well as the oil filter and air filter – to protect the new oil. Every 3000 kilometres (1860 miles) can be taken as a general guide for the frequency of oil changes, although this information should be in the bike's handbook.

This figure is quite low, especially when compared to that for cars. This is largely because motorcycles of all but the smallest engine sizes are basically high performance machines and the engine is often revved in excess of 7000 rpm – thus the oil really gets a hammering.

Aside from regular changes of filter, the oil within an engine can be protected by using the choke as little as possible and warming the machine up from cold as quickly as possible. This will reduce oil dilution, and start the oil flowing quicker.

It is also possible to 'improve' the oil a little by going for a long fast run, as the high temperatures will burn off some of the oil dilutants.

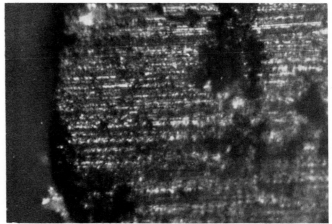

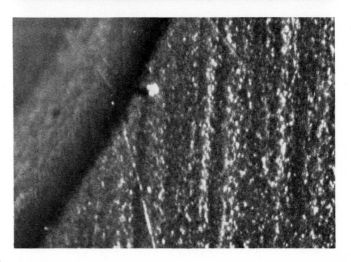

Top: An ugly example of piston seizure. Metal has smeared over the rings.

Centre: The rough, corroded edge of a piston ring seen under a microscope.

Bottom: Wear and corrosion on a valve guide, barely visible to the naked eye.

Two-stroke lubrication

Positive pump feed lubrication has helped make modern two-strokes the successful everyday commuter transport for thousands of riders. But to many owners the operation of this lubrication system is a complete mystery.

Fortunately, the two-stroke [cycle] oil pump is a very reliable device, but it still needs an understanding of its operation to keep it working correctly.

Basically the pump adjusts the oil feed to the crankshaft or inlet tract, or both – depending on the bike – to suit the engine revs and throttle opening. So, the wider the throttle or the higher the revs the more oil is pumped.

On Jawas, CZs, Yamahas, Harley-Davidsons and some Kawasakis, oil is drawn from the tank, usually situated behind one of the side panels or underneath the seat, and fed by the pump direct to the carburettor manifold. On Suzukis and most multi-cylinder Kawasakis oil is also pumped into the main bearings, from where it feeds the big-ends through holes in the flywheels.

All the pumps used on Suzuki, Yamaha, Kawasaki and even the Italian-built Harley-Davidson two-strokes are made in Japan by Mikuni, and the Jawa/CZ pumps are similar to the Yamaha pump, so the basic principle is the same in all. A worm gear driven from the crank or a gearbox shaft turns a shaft in a cylinder that is the oil pump body. The shaft has a cam profile on the end of it which butts up against a fixed pin in the cylinder, so that as the shaft rotates it moves up and down in its bore.

This up and down motion gives the shaft a plunger action to provide the pumping force. Through recesses or holes drilled through the other end of the rotating piston/shaft, oil is sucked into the pump, pressurised, and pumped out again. The faster the motor turns, the faster the rate of pumping, and hence the oil flow.

The stroke

The stroke of the pump (how far the cam pushes it up and down the cylinder) is governed by another cam which butts up against a stop on the end of the piston when the throttle is closed. When the throttle is opened, the cable turns the pump pulley, or lever arm, which in turn rotates the cam away from the stop, allowing the piston to use its full stroke. There are detail differences from pump to pump, and some have complicated refinements, but the basic principles are the same for all.

Oil pumps are usually very reliable, and do not need servicing. If a pump does become faulty it will probably have to be replaced as they are not usually repairable.

The basic checks which have to be made on the lubrication system are to keep the oil topped up, the pump correctly adjusted and bled, and all the pipes secure and unkinked. Make sure the pump is firmly fixed in place, but avoid overtightening the mounting bolts because you may warp the body, causing a loss of oil pressure, or you may even make the worm drive gears bind together. Bolts holding the oil lines onto the pump and crankcase or carburettor manifold should be checked for security periodically, but again beware of overtightening, because the bolts are hollow to allow the oil to pass through them and can easily snap off. If the oil pipes have to be removed for any reason always replace the sealing washers with factory-supplied ones.

Always keep the tank topped up. If the oil level drops low enough for one bubble of air to get into the feed line and you do not spot it in time, trouble will ensue. This is because all pumps depend on the non-compressibility of the oil to operate, and a bubble of air will most likely stop the oil flow completely.

When you do top up the tank, make sure no dirt or grit gets in. Lastly, ensure that the pump is adjusted at the specified service intervals because oil pump cables stretch and can eventually rob the engine of the correct quantity of oil.

Top: Overtightening an oil pump can lead to distortion and faulty operation.

Bottom: Leaking seals can be replaced but the system has to be bled at the pump.

CZ/Jawa

Newer CZ and Jawa machines all use the 'Posilube' lubrication system. The way this operates is that oil from a tank, mounted on the left of the machine, is gravity fed to the pump – which is driven by the crankshaft and situated in the left casing, behind a screw-mounted cover. The oil is pumped past a non-return valve into the inlet manifold where it mixes with the fuel/air mixture to lubricate the big-end, small-end and cylinder. The mains are lubricated by transmission oil.

There is a slight difference on the 350 twin which feeds its oil into the top of the carburettor where it is fed into the charge through a static hollow needle.

The Czech bikes have a unique throttle cable pump operation, where the throttle cable goes straight to the oil pump pulley and another cable comes from the other side of the pulley to the carburettor. This system makes setting up the pump pulley adjustment a bit more awkward than on other bikes, because every time you adjust one cable to get the carburettor slide sitting on the throttle-stop screw, or the pump pulley marks lined up, or throttle free play correct, it is likely to throw out the adjustment on everything else. The best method is to adjust the throttle-to-pump cable so that the pulley mark lines up with the ridge on the pump body when the throttle is shut; and then adjust the pump-to-carb cable so that there is 1mm (.004in) slack in the cable at the carburettor end when the slide is sitting on the throttle-stop screw.

Should you remove the pump for any reason, or get air into the system, you must bleed it thoroughly after topping up the oil tank.

First remove the bleed screw – the one that is most obvious once the pump cover is removed and turn the plastic wheel clockwise with the throttle held fully open until oil pours out of the hole in a steady stream with no air bubbles, and no bubbles are left visible in the transparent pipe from the tank.

Put the screw back in its hole with a new washer and then disconnect the oil pipe where it joins the crankcase, and turn the plastic wheel again until all the air bubbles are bled out. Put the pipe back on and start the engine, watching the pipes to see if any more air bubbles appear. One air bubble in the pipe may not hinder the oil flow, but try to get it bled out if at all possible, to be on the safe side.

Yamaha

The Yamaha 'Autolube' pump-fed oil-injection system is a simpler design than some. The pump is driven by the crankshaft on the right side of the engine and is metered by a cable run round a pulley operated by the throttle. A junction box under the fuel tank converts one throttle cable into two carburettor cables and one pump cable. One pipe feeds the pump with oil from the tank and two more take the oil under pressure from the pump to the carburettor inlet manifolds. Adjustment is quite simple, but has recently changed because Yamaha altered the mode of pump adjustment at the end of 1975.

Up to and including 1975 the pump was adjusted by altering the cable adjuster at the pump end so that the 'pip' on the pump pulley lined up with the guide pin with the throttle closed. Pumps on newer machines require the pip and pin to line up with throttle fully open. Be sure of your pump type before adjusting it, for if you set your 1976 model the 1975 way, the bike will make a lot of smoke.

The stroke of the pump on Yamahas can be measured and adjusted by the owner. Slowly turn the plastic wheel, on the

Top: On Jawa/CZ machines this plastic wheel is provided for bleeding the oil pump at two different points.

Bottom: The Yamaha oil pump has to have the stroke set to the correct height via the shims under this plate.

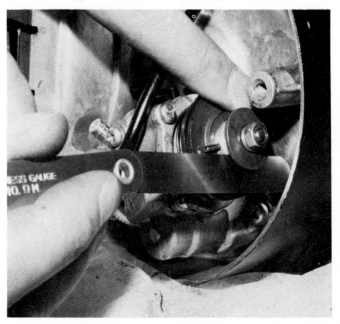

left end of the pump, clockwise until the plate on the far right end of the pump lifts away from the pulley. Keeping the throttle closed, you then measure this gap with a feeler gauge. It should be .20 to .25mm (.080 to .100in) and you adjust it by adding or subtracting .10mm (.040in) shims underneath the plate. All adjustments to the pump stroke or pulley setting should be made after the carburettor(s) have been synchronised and the throttle cable adjusted. This is because, if you adjust the throttle cable afterwards, it may alter the pump setting.

The lubrication system should be bled of all air at periodic maintenance intervals, as well as when the pump is removed or the oil level in the tank runs low.

The pump is bled in a similar way to the CZ method. Remove the bleed screw, next to the main feed pipe, open the throttle fully and turn the plastic wheel until bubble-free oil pours out of the hole. Refit screw and keep turning the wheel until oil issues steadily from the carburettor feed lines. Again, make a visual check of the translucent oil lines for bubbles.

Kawasaki

The Kawasaki 'Supalube' and 'Injectolube' systems feed the carburettor manifold plus crankshaft respectively using a pump that is a more elongated version of the Yamaha and CZ/Jawa units but working in basically the same way. The pump is located in the front right hand casing on most models and is driven by a gear from the crankshaft. There are no little plastic wheels on these pumps so bleeding the system is made a little easier. Again this must be done after pump removal, or running down to a low oil tank level. Most of the work of bleeding the system is done by the engine. Let it run at idle while you hold the pump quadrant [cable connector] fully open for a couple of minutes, by which time there should be no air bubbles left in the translucent pipes from pump to crank-cases. While this method is easier, it has the drawback of producing clouds of blue smoke.

Pump adjustment should be carried out only after the carburettor(s) have been set up properly, and the throttle cable adjusted at the handlebar end. Then, keeping the throttle shut, screw the pump cable adjuster in or out until the first mark on the pump quadrant [cable connectors] lines up with the index mark on the pump body. There is a full-throttle mark on most quadrants as well, but it is better to use the closed-throttle line as it usually lines up more accurately.

There are no strokes to measure or shims to manipulate on these pumps, so if the pump is working well leave it alone. A useful point to note is that the rev-counter [tachometer] drive is taken off the same gear as the pump, so if the counter stops your oil pump may have no drive either. If this happens pull up immediately and find out why, otherwise you could risk wrecking the motor.

Suzuki

There is little doubt that Suzuki employ the most comprehensive lubrication system on their two-stroke machines. They use a system called CCI – Crankshaft Cylinder Injection – and that is exactly what it does, ensuring that all the major bearing surfaces are adequately lubricated. Some of the bigger Suzukis also have a feature called SRIS – Suzuki Recycle Injection System – which takes excess oil from the bottom of the crankcase and spits it back into the cylinder. This means that there is no build-up of oil to smoke out of the silencers.

Again, the pump should need no maintenance, apart from adjusting the throttle cam setting periodically. There are two ways of doing this. Ignore the dots on the lever arm and line

up the scribe mark with the register on the pump body when the throttle is fully open, or when the dot on the carburettor slide is at the upper part of the carburettor alignment hole. On the Suzuki models which have this carburettor alignment facility, the hole in the carburettor body is hidden by a screw-in inspection plug. Whichever method you use, it is advisable to adjust the throttle cable free play and carburettor synchronization before the pump setting, because then you are sure of not disturbing the pump setting afterwards.

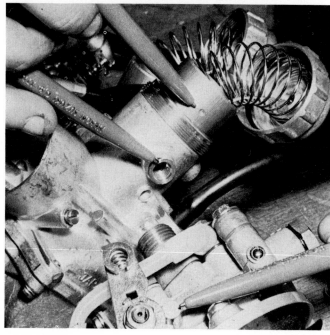

Top: Maintenance of the Kawasaki oil pump is just a simple cable adjustment.

Bottom: The Suzuki oil pump adjustment sounds more complicated than it is. Here are the dots and marks to line up.

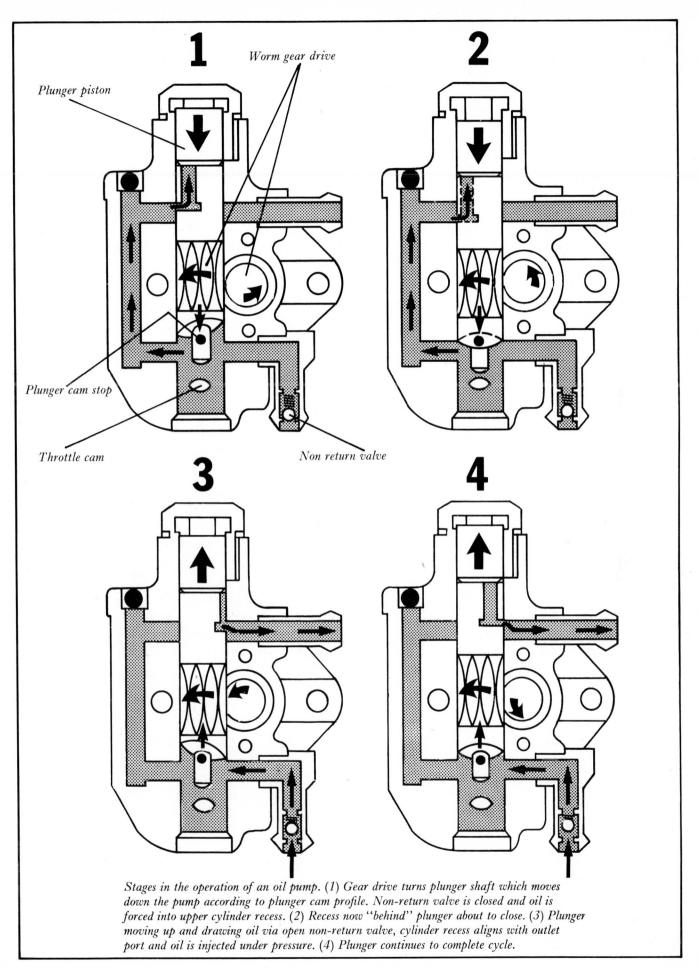

1

Worm gear drive

Plunger piston

Plunger cam stop

Throttle cam

Non return valve

2

3

4

Stages in the operation of an oil pump. (1) Gear drive turns plunger shaft which moves down the pump according to plunger cam profile. Non-return valve is closed and oil is forced into upper cylinder recess. (2) Recess now "behind" plunger about to close. (3) Plunger moving up and drawing oil via open non-return valve, cylinder recess aligns with outlet port and oil is injected under pressure. (4) Plunger continues to complete cycle.

Bleeding the system after a rebuild is done by first loosening the bolt which holds the inlet pipe onto the pump, letting oil flow out until there are no air bubbles left, and then re-tightening the bolt. This is speedily followed by bleeding the pump and lines, while running the engine at idling speed with the pump lever arm held fully open by hand.

A relatively new innovation from Suzuki is an oil flow meter, which is simply a calibrated burette which you fix into the tank-to-pump line and check the flow rate at different throttle openings. For the home merchant, however, there is little value in owning this tool.

Problems with the lubrication system are rare, but occasionally there is a sticking non-return ball valve resulting in air getting into the system, or a sticking pump lever – which is usually indicated by smoke pouring from the exhaust pipes. Both problems are usually due to use of transmission oil or something similar, instead of the SAE 30 non-diluent two-stroke oil that is recommended. In the same way as on the Kawasaki, the rev-counter drives off the same gear as the oil pump, so a broken tachometer may mean there is no oil running through the engine.

Harley-Davidson
On Harley-Davidsons, which also use Japanese pumps, the pump's location is variable. It can be either in the right crank-case cover or behind the gearbox sprocket. It is driven by the crankshaft or gearbox, drawing oil from the tank which can be in the top tube or in a plastic container under the petrol tank. The oil filler cap on both types is at the front of the petrol tank, the level being measured either by a plastic dip-stick or by peering under the fuel tank.

The pump feeds the carburettor intake through a non-return valve to stop crankcase pressure blowback down the pipe. Pump and carburettor control cables are connected to the throttle through an equaliser, but the Harleys do have the refinement of an oil filter in the line connection at the tank which should be inspected and cleaned periodically. The pump should not be dismantled for repairs. If it stops working you must throw it away and fit a new one.

The pump is correctly adjusted when the maximum flow mark – the line furthest away from the stop position – lines up with the reference mark on the pump body with throttle fully open. Adjust by the cable sleeve at the pump end. The position of the pump quadrant [cable connector] should be checked periodically and reset after altering the throttle cable adjustment.

To bleed the system, remove the oil pipe from the carburettor manifold banjo, drain the fuel tank and put about one pint [0.57 litre] of 50:1 fuel mix into the tank to lubricate the motor while bleeding. Start the engine and run at idle speed, while holding the pump quadrant [cable connector] at its full-flow position, until bubble-free oil flows out of the feed pipe and no bubbles are visible in the pipes.

Oil pump on the American Harley-Davidson is actually made in Japan by Mikuni so it is not surprising that adjustment procedure is similar to Japanese machines.

Carbon clean~out

Carbon build up in a two-stroke [cycle] engine can reduce the efficiency of the engine to the point where it is using a lot more fuel than it needs to. Add to this a loss of engine power under full load and there is a good case for regular engine decarbonization.

The worst offender for collecting carbon is the exhaust system. It is also the most difficult part to keep clear. This is because a lot of oil and fuel is pumped into the hot exhaust where it is burned onto the inside of the pipe and around the baffles. Before making a start on cleaning out the exhaust pipe it will have to be removed from the machine. Always start at the exhaust port and remove the fixing bolts or locking ring before slackening off any other mountings. Most trail bikes have their exhaust systems made all in one piece, whereas most road machines have a separate pipe and silencer.

Cleaning the silencer

Having removed the silencer from the machine the next problem is removing the carbon from the inside. Many two-stroke [cycle] exhaust systems have detachable baffles and these should be removed first. You may have some trouble in freeing the baffles because carbon builds up around the joints and you may need to heat them before they will come free. The baffles on most Japanese bikes are retained by a single screw located near the end of the tail pipe.

To clean the system out, start by washing the baffles and the inside of the silencer with a good de-greaser to remove the wet sticky oil, and then allow to dry. The hard carbon deposits can be removed from the baffles with a stiff wire brush. To remove the deposits inside the silencer, caustic soda is usually employed to burn out the carbon, but a lot of care must be taken with this substance – do not get it in your eyes or on your skin. Start with a bucket of water and slowly add the caustic soda until you have a saturated solution that will absorb no more crystals. Next, plug the end of the silencer, and pour the solution into the pipe and leave it for 24 hours. This should effectively loosen all hardened deposits.

Cleaning the engine

Carbon also builds up in the engine, and the head should be removed. It is normally only retained by four studs and nuts, which also hold down the barrel. Carbon from the head and top of the piston can be removed with a piece of wood sharpened to make a scraper. The head and piston can then be polished with wire wool to remove all final traces of carbon after the worst has been scraped off.

After the piston has been cleaned the barrel can be removed. Start by lifting it a couple of inches and then cover the base of the barrel to prevent any dirt from entering the crankcase. The barrel can now safely be lifted off. Ideally you should remove the piston from the con-rod for cleaning up the ring grooves. Many current machines have their circlips made from thin spring wire and removing them usually leads to their being distorted, so use new circlips on replacement. Alternatively, you could leave the piston in place on the connecting rod, and just clean the piston crown.

Top: The exhaust port is a prime collector of carbon. Stubborn deposits can be removed with a wire wheel.

Bottom: Carbon deposits around the head can cause pre-ignition and piston damage.

Removing the piston rings

To clean out the ring grooves the piston rings will have to be removed. This is done by opening them out with the ends of your thumbs, just enough to enable them to be lifted over the top of the piston crown. All carbon should be removed from the ring grooves using an old ring, which has been broken and filed into a scraper. Final polishing can be carried out using a piece of string soaked in engine oil. The piston rings on a two-stroke act as the valves in that they control the covering and uncovering of the ports; as well as controlling the combustion pressure, and the crankcase compression. Thus they are vital to the general well-being of the engine and they should be renewed if at all suspect. Be very careful when refitting the rings to ensure that you fit them the right way up. Most modern engines use a 'Keystone' type ring and this has an obvious top and bottom on it.

The cylinder barrel should be cleaned next. The transfer and inlet ports will have very little carbon or lacquer in them and the majority of work will be confined to the exhaust port. The build-up here can be quite bad and if your barrel is a cast iron one, then a wire brush mounted in an electric drill is the best way to remove it. If the barrel is of the cast alloy type, then a wire brush in a drill will severely damage the inside of the port – so you will have to scrape it out the hard way, with a sharp piece of wood or plastic such as an old toothbrush handle.

Having removed all carbon from the engine's internals it should be reassembled. With the rings refitted to the piston and the piston fitted to the connecting rod, (with new cir-clips), the rings have to be compressed as the barrel is fitted. This can be achieved on most engines with the fingers, squeezing the rings into the bore as the barrel is lowered. It is vital that you line up the rings so that their ends locate on the small peg in the ring groove. This peg is there to prevent the ring from turning on the piston and springing into any of the ports.

You can sometimes get away with re-using a base gasket, but the head and exhaust gaskets should be replaced every time. When refitting the head use a torque wrench, tightening the nuts alternately, a little at a time, until you reach the required setting.

Top left: If the barrels are lifted for cleaning, block the crankcase mouths.

Left: Silencer baffles can be cleaned in de-greaser or with a wire brush.

Above: Badly clogged baffles may need caustic soda or burning with a blowlamp.

General Servicing

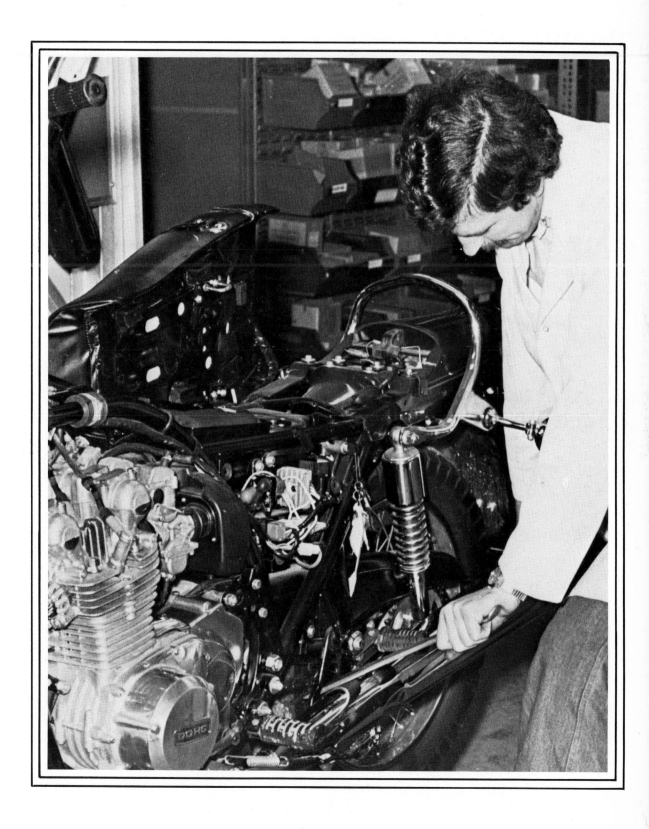

Routine maintenance

Preventive maintenance is only part of the function of servicing, because good and regular attention will extend the life of the bike's internals and in the long term add to its secondhand retail value.

Service intervals

Service intervals are usually based on a system of time or distance over which the various components on a motorcycle should be checked. When carrying out a service be systematic in your approach. If you start working on one part of the bike and then move quickly to another, something will be missed and it will be this very item that lets you down on the road, making the whole schedule a waste of time. Check the service chart and then work through the list – in this way you will not miss anything.

Lubrication

Most services start with the lubrication system, and draining the oil is normally the first task. There are two points to watch: firstly, you should have the engine hot, as this will allow the old oil to flow freely; and secondly, make sure that you do not over tighten the drain plug when re-fitting. Modern engines usually have alloy cases and the hexagonal nut on the drain plug is often much bigger than it needs to be. Thus it is easy to overtighten the plug, especially with a large ring spanner [wrench].

Having drained the oil the filter should not be neglected. On some machines this will take the form of a strainer which has to be removed and washed clean with solvent or fuel and left to dry. On later bikes you will find a paper-leaf filter, as used on cars, which should be changed as recommended by the manufacturer. Do not try to save money by attempting to clean a filter of this type. You will be wasting your time and the life of the engine will be shortened.

Always try to use the grade of oil recommended by the manufacturer even if you prefer to use a different brand. Many machines are now listed as needing a 10/40 oil, but if this is not readily available you can compromise by using a 20/50 in the summer and a straight 10/30 for the winter. The thinner oil is needed in the winter because engines generally take longer to warm up and tend to run cooler.

Drive chain maintenance

Drive chain maintenance is possibly one of the most overlooked routine jobs. Yet this should be one of the most frequent services carried out on a motorcycle.

Maintenance takes three forms: lubrication, checking for wear and retensioning.

Lubrication

If the chain is looking rather dry and rusty a quick run over with an oil-can may make it look better, but it will do little to preserve the chain. This is because the vital areas of the chain, in between the bushes and rollers, will not be lubricated.

An aerosol containing a special chain grease, however, is more likely to lubricate these areas if directed carefully between the side plates. This method also has the advantage of being quick and clean.

Possibly the best method though, in terms of perfect chain lubrication and hence increasing chain life, is the grease bath. This involves removing the chain (for which you may need a chain-splitter if there is no spring link) washing it in fuel or paraffin, and then placing it in a bath of grease which has been heated to make it fluid.

While this is a rather long and unpleasant job when compared to using an aerosol, it offers a much greater degree of protection from wear and the grease is usually more resistant to being washed off by the rain.

Generally a chain should be given a grease bath treatment every 2000 miles, as well as being regularly lubricated with an aerosol grease.

Checking for wear

Chain wear can be detected easily in several ways. With the chain removed first, give it a visual check for wear or damage. Next, try to coil the chain, letting it fold up under its own weight. This operation will reveal any 'sticky' links which can then be more closely inspected.

Another test is to stretch the chain out in a straight line with the side plates vertical. Try to bend the chain away from the line sideways. If you can do this by more than 15cm (00in) then it will soon need replacing as it is worn.

Chains are sold in pitch sizes as well as length. Pitch length being the distance between the centres of the pins. By measuring a number of pitches and working out how long it should be, you can assess the stretch. As an example, if the pitch is 13mm ($\frac{1}{2}$in), 20 pitches should measure 254mm (10in). If it is more than 260mm (10$\frac{1}{4}$in) the chain will need replacing.

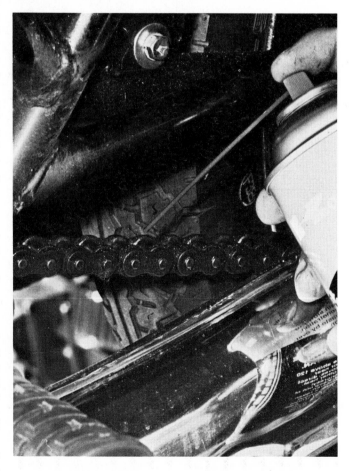

Regular adjustment and lubrication will prolong chain life.

Chain retensioning

As a chain is used it will stretch and become slack. A slack chain will wear the sprocket teeth, therefore it is essential that the correct chain tension is maintained.

Most chains are at the correct tension when it is possible to move the chain about 19mm (¾in) up and down in between the sprockets. An overtight chain is as bad as one too slack, so when readjusting the tension do not be tempted to overdo it.

Adjustment usually involves first slackening off the axle nut and possibly the brake linkage. Then, the wheel adjuster lock-nuts can be undone and the adjusters screwed in to force the wheel back. When the chain is at the correct tension retighten the locknuts and recheck the tension.

When turning the adjusters be sure to turn them both by the same amount. Usually there are marks on the frame for reference. If you turn one adjuster more than the other, the wheel alignment will be altered. You can check for this by spinning the wheel, while the bike is on its stand, and watching it for trueness.

Chain adjustment will usually need doing every 300 miles but this figure varies a great deal from one bike to another.

Plugs

Next, check the spark-plugs or plugs. This can be done with the engine still warm as the head will have expanded. The latter makes removal a little bit easier, and reduces the risk of damaging a plug thread. If you change a plug be sure that you refit the correct grade plug. On a two-stroke [cycle] this is vital as the wrong plug in a high performance two-stroke engine can burn through a piston.

Having removed the plugs they can be cleaned at a garage by sand blasting or, as long as you are careful, you can clean them up yourself with a soft wire brush.

After cleaning the plug, check that the gap is set to the maker's specification for your machine and visually check on the state of electrode wear. The two electrodes should be clean and sharp without having any rounded appearance to the edges. When setting the gap try to resist the temptation of banging the plug on its end to close the gap. The correct way of doing it is to lever the earth [ground] electrode into position.

Contact points

Contact points are next on the list. Some high performance two- and four-stroke engines are fitted with electronic ignition which replaces the contact breaker points system. This type of ignition is usually maintenance-free, but best left alone by the home mechanic.

Two-stroke engines are normally fitted with one set of points per cylinder in the engine, but four-strokes can be arranged so that two cylinders share the same set of points. If you consult your handbook it will probably tell you the arrangement on your machine, as well as the points gap, at full lift of the breaker cam. This value will be a range, rather than a specific figure. The reason for this lack of accurate data is that the points gap only helps to determine the time that the points are together. This 'dwell angle' is the important factor, not the amount that the points are lifted apart. Before setting the points gap, check the points for dirt and pitting and clean as necessary with a points file or emery cloth.

In order to set the points dwell angle perfectly, you will have to use a special meter called a dwell-meter. This meter is attached across the points and measures the operating period while the engine is running. However, simply setting the points gap halfway between the two given values, using a feeler gauge to measure the gap at its widest, gives an adequate setting.

Top: With points fully open adjust the fixed point to give correct gap.

Bottom: Loosening the clamp screw and moving backplate adjusts the timing.

31

Ignition timing

Having ensured that the points are in good condition and are opening as they should, you now have to arrange for them to open, and deliver the ignition spark, at the right time. Ignition timing methods vary from one machine to another in detail but broadly speaking they follow two basic principles.

Static ignition timing (mainly two-stroke machines) is the setting of the points opening position with the engine fixed in the correct position. A piston position measurement is usually given and a dial gauge is used to set the piston at this predetermined figure. The exact setting will vary with different engines but it usually lies around 2 to 3mm (.008in to .012in) before top dead centre. Using an accurate measuring device down the plug hole, such as a dial gauge, the piston position is set to this figure and then the points are moved around the breaker cam until they just start to open. This points opening position is normally determined with the aid of a meter or light bulb wired across the points.

The other method of ignition timing, mainly used on four-stroke machines is that of connecting a special timing light into the high tension circuit. The timing light is triggered by the ignition system and so flashes when the engine fires. By aiming the light at a mark on the engine's crankshaft the mark appears to 'freeze' under the strobe effect. This mark should line up next to a static mark on a nearby casing if the timing is correct. If not the points will have to be moved round the cam until it does.

Whichever system you have to use with your engine it must be repeated once for every set of points that you have. If your machine is a three cylinder two-stroke then you have to time the engine as though it were three single cylinder units. It is obvious that you must work very accurately, or the timing will not be identical for each of the cylinders and power will be lost.

Valve adjustment

Valve adjustment or tappet adjustment (as it is more often, but incorrectly, known) is a quite simple operation. The valve clearance which is adjusted, is a specific amount of play in the valve operation which is required to effect the correct timing of the valves. This clearance does not have to be at the tip of the valve stem. On some engines the clearance is set between the camshaft lobe and the follower. The clearance is primarily there to give the correct timing to the valve gear. It is not to allow for any expansion in the valve train as the engine heats up. Some engines have to have their tappets set with the engine hot, so any expansion will already have taken place. Incorrect tappet clearance will result in incorrect timing of the valve train and loss of performance. A tappet with zero clearance will hold a valve off its seat and burn it out in the valve seat area.

The adjustment procedure varies so much from one machine to another and you should follow the system laid out in the manual which relates to your machine – and your machine only.

Carburettors

Carburettor adjustment is quite simple on a single-cylinder engine but tends to be extremely complex on those engines with several carburettors. Refer to the later chapter on carburettors which explains how adjustment should be done.

Brakes

Brakes and braking are covered in a later chapter. Do not forget that the brakes are more important than the engine and their servicing should not be neglected.

Steering

Steering head bearings are easily overlooked, yet their adjustment is very simple. If you have any play in the head races this can be adjusted by means of the collar, which is located under the top yoke of the forks. It is often necessary to slacken the top yoke centre nut before moving the adjuster around with a 'C' spanner [wrench]. After adjustment the forks should not be so tight that they cannot fall from side to side under their own weight.

The remaining service checks are mainly weekly ones rather than specific service items, that is, lights, horn, battery and tyre pressures.

It should be noted that the service chart in this book is only a guide to regular servicing. For exact details on the recommended service intervals for any particular machine you should consult your local main dealer who should be able to supply a handbook direct from the manufacturer.

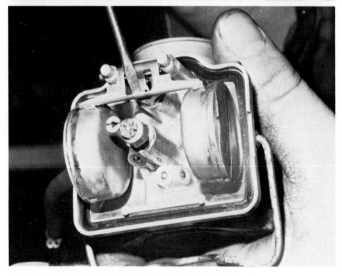

Top: Steering head bearings are adjusted by this ring nut, after loosening locknut.

Bottom: Carburettor float height can be altered by bending the float arm slightly.

Moped

Servicing a moped is pretty much the same as servicing any motorcycle. Don't make the mistake of thinking that a small capacity, low power output engine will not need complicated maintenance. If your machine is a two-stroke you will need the same equipment for setting up the timing as you would for a much bigger bike. A dial gauge and points meter are essential.

The cycle parts of the machine, brakes etc., are fairly straightforward and most of the adjustments can be carried out using the tool kit supplied with the bike. If you are not sure of the procedure do not play around with the brakes. If you make a mistake with the engine it could cost you money, if you make a mistake with the brakes it could cost you your life.

The picture sequence that follows is only a guide to servicing since similar operations will vary greatly from one make of machine to another. Basic service operations are normally explained in the manufacturer's handbook. If a particular operation is not listed then do not attempt it without seeking expert advice.

The gearbox oil is normally drained with the engine hot so that the oil flows more readily.

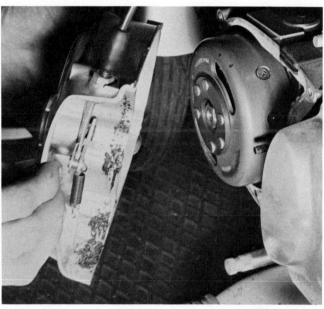

Most mopeds have flywheel generators incorporating the ignition system contact breaker points.

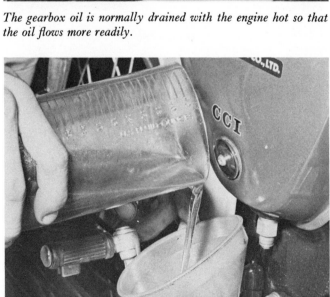

It is essential to use the correct grade of oil for long gearbox life. Check your handbook.

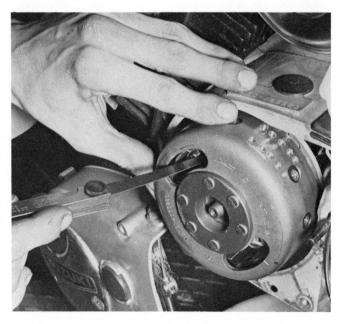

The points gap can be checked through this slot in the flywheel. There is no need to remove it.

If the points are in very bad condition and new ones are needed you will have to pull off the rotor.

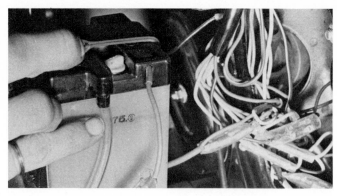

When checking your battery make sure that the breather pipe exits well clear of the machine.

After removing the centre nut you will have to use a special tool to break the taper joint.

For timing the ignition on a two-stroke you must have a dial gauge and points meter or bleeper.

Some mopeds have backplate screws (circled) for ignition timing adjustment. For others, adjust gap.

On this model, oil pump setting is checked by first lining up this dot on the carburettor slide.

Contact point faces will only take a certain amount of cleaning up. If in doubt, renew them.

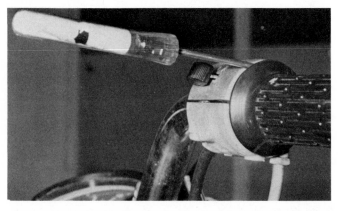

To hold the carburettor slide at the required position, wedge the twist grip open with a screwdriver.

Once this has been done you simply adjust the oil pump cable until the two marks line up.

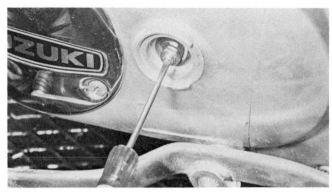

Clutch adjustment is not always carried out at the handlebar cable adjuster. See your handbook.

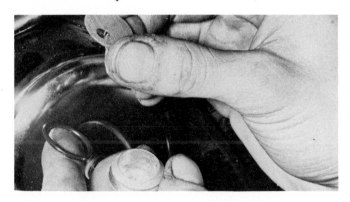

Most fuel taps have a filter in some form or another, either here or in the fuel tank.

Brake adjustment is normally via a simple cable. Use the indicator to keep an eye on brake wear.

Carburettor mixture screws normally have a basic setting from the fully closed position.

If you ignore the brake wear indicator you may end up with scored drums like this one.

On a small moped it is essential to keep the exhaust pipe free from any carbon build up.

Having taken the brake apart you can lubricate the cams with a high melting point grease.

2-strokes

While two-strokes are basically very simple they still need careful maintenance and, in some areas this can be quite critical. Ignition timing, spark plug grade and condition etc, can have serious effects on high performance engines, ultimately burning a hole in a piston. Special equipment, such as a dial gauge and ohm-meter, is often necessary to adjust the ignition timing. Without the right equipment there is an even chance of making matters worse – so if you don't have the tools for the job, get a dealer to do it for you.

Most servicing points can be tackled by an owner with an average tool kit. Often the bike's tool kit will just about be good enough. The picture sequence shows typical points which will need attention. While it is obviously worth consulting the maker's handbook or shop manual for recommended settings, lubricants, etc, remember that these are generalised recommendations. For instance, in dirty or dusty weather conditions air cleaners and drive chains will need more frequent attention than if the bike is used in finer weather.

Keep the tank topped up with a recommended grade of two-stroke oil, not a multigrade.

Check that the starter jet is not sticking and that the carburettor top is tightened.

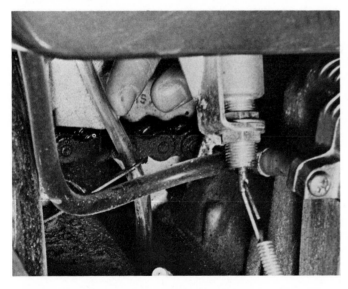

Letting tank run low could allow air bubbles into the oil line, cutting off supply.

Electrical connections must be sound, particularly earthing points like this.

Make sure there is a good exhaust seal – a leak here could cause engine damage.

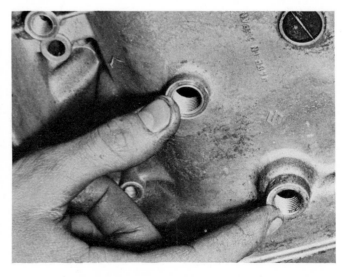

Take care when draining oil – one plug locates the gear selector plunger!

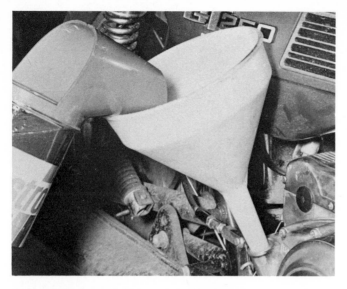

The wrong grade of oil can cause clutch drag – check with the handbook first.

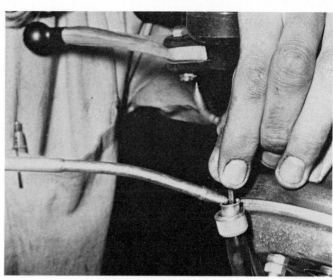

Wrong! Instrument cables should be greased as oil can get into the instrument heads.

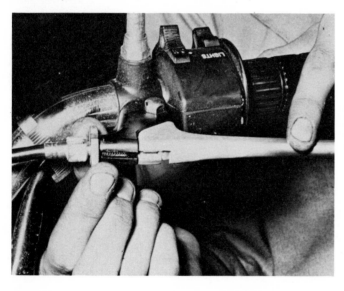

The clutch cable adjuster should be set to give about 2mm play at the lever.

To inspect the air cleaner element it may be necessary to remove the complete box.

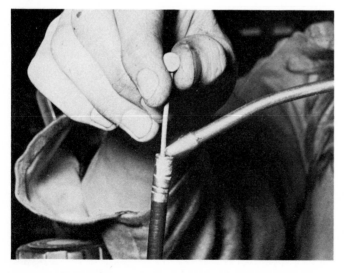

Regular cable lubrication ensures smooth controls. Make sure the oil penetrates.

The air cleaner box will be screwed or clipped together, locating a paper . . .

. . . or sponge element inside. Paper types can be blown clean using an airline.

Always use the adjusters to pull the wheel back to adjust the chain, keeping chain tight.

Most exhausts have a detachable baffle to aid cleaning, held by a small set screw.

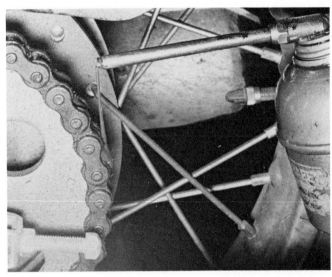

Frequent lubrication is essential to protect chains, particularly in dirty conditions.

Feeling for uneven exhaust pulses can show up out-of-synchronisation carburettors.

Check all carburettor fittings and look carefully for leaks around the intake.

If exhausts get clogged with carbon deposits engine performance may suffer badly.

Check the points condition, renewing when the faces are pitted, and reset gap.

Checking tyre pressures and tyre condition should be a weekly operation.

Adjust the points gap using the correct feeler gauge with the cam on full lift.

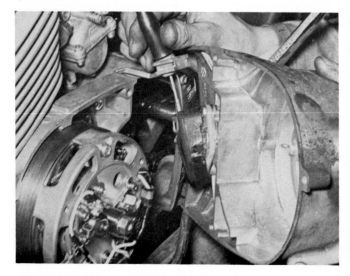

Inspect the clutch operating mechanism and keep the pivot well greased.

Timing is often critical and should be adjusted using a dial gauge to set engine.

Keep the brake master cylinder topped up and change the fluid every 12-18 months.

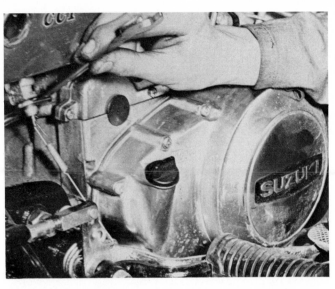

The stop-light switch is held with a screw and locknut to give adjustment.

Adjust drum brakes – checking the wear indicator – and reset stop-light switch.

Swing arm bearings are sometimes fitted with a grease nipple. Pump grease right through.

The wear adjuster shows when the brake linings have worn down to their limit.

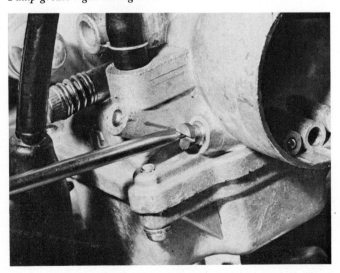

When everything else has been set, warm up engine and adjust carburettor idle settings.

4-strokes

While four-strokes have the extra complications of valve gear and re-circulating oil systems, they are not usually more difficult to work on than two-stroke engines. The majority of the servicing points will be similar to two-strokes, as the picture sequence shows.

In addition there will be valve clearances to set and cam chain adjustment to be made. As these points can be critical to the well-being of the engine, it is essential to follow the maker's instructions.

Whether the motor has dry sump (oil carried in a separate oil tank) or wet sump (oil carried inside the crankcase) lubrication, it will be necessary to drain the oil at the recommended interval, preferably after a longish run when the oil is hot and will flow more freely. At each, or every other oil change, the oil filter should also be renewed.

Many four-stroke multi-cylinder machines have to have their carburettors balanced so that they idle and run smoothly. Without extensive experience, this can only be done accurately with vacuum gauges connected to adaptors on the carburettor stubs. With the engine idling, each carburettor throttle stop is adjusted until all the gauges read the same, the final idling speed being set on the master throttle control or cable adjuster.

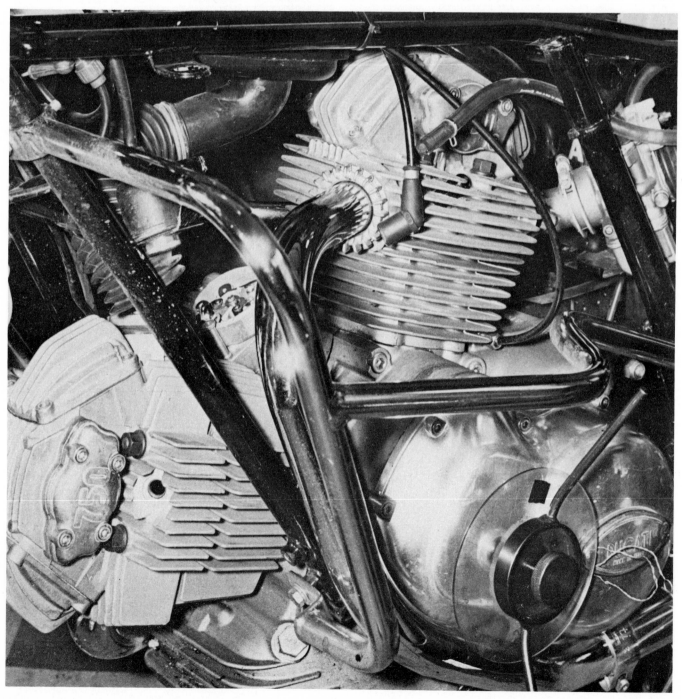

On metal-type plug caps this sealing ring must be in place and in good condition.

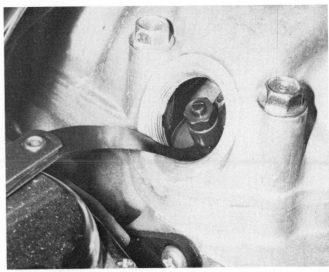

Some tappets are very awkward to get at but you can distort the feeler gauge, shown here.

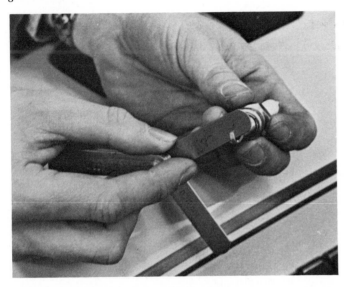

Spark plugs should be cleaned by sand-blasting and the gap kept to specification.

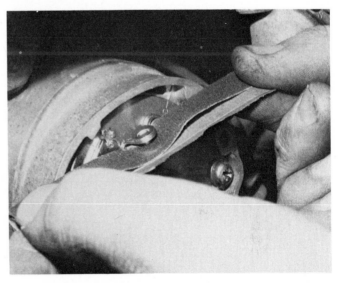

How to clean the points. Do not overdo it, or the face will be damaged.

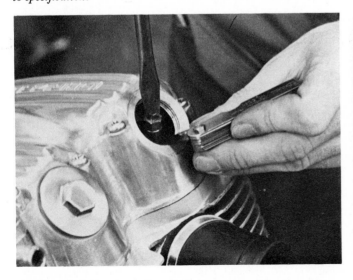

Tappet adjustment is vital so check your manual for the sequence of adjustment.

With the contact breaker at full lift, the gap is adjusted after cleaning up the faces.

Most four-strokes are timed with a strobe light which flashes with the spark.

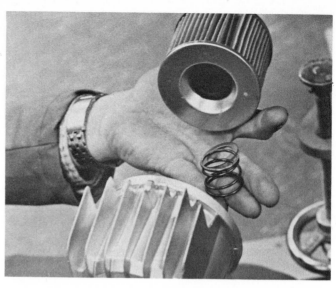

Your engine's kidney, the oil filter, must be changed at the recommended intervals.

This appears to "freeze" the timing marks. Advance mechanism can be lightly oiled.

Some units have a gauze-type filter which requires cleaning to prevent sludge build-up.

Engine oil should be drained when the engine is hot. This allows the oil to flow freely.

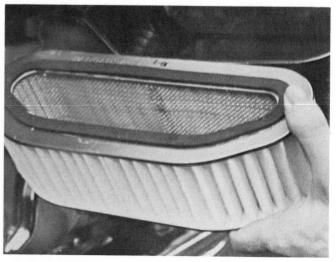

A dirty air filter will make the mixture richer, wasting fuel and increasing engine wear.

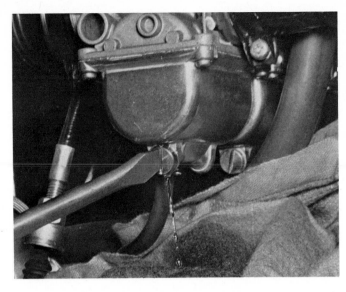

An important service job: draining down the float bowls to remove sediment.

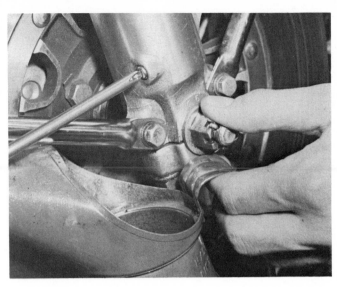

Front fork fluid drain screw. Pump the forks up and down to remove fluid.

If in doubt then leave it to a dealer. Mixture adjustment is a little less critical.

Where the front fork oil goes in. Each leg must be re-filled with the correct oil.

Multi-carb balancing can be a real headache unless you have vacuum gauges like this.

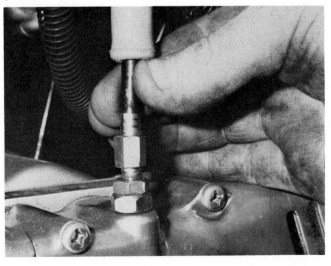

Clutch push-rod adjustment should not be attempted until the cable as been slackened.

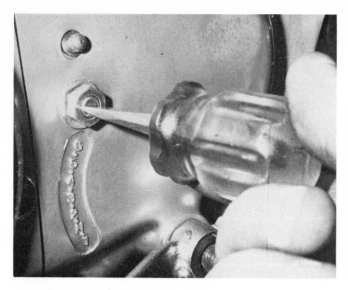

Clutch push rod adjustment is a three-minute job. It is often neglected.

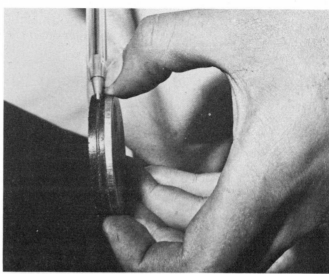

Pads are marked differently, some having a thin red line, others a step to indicate wear.

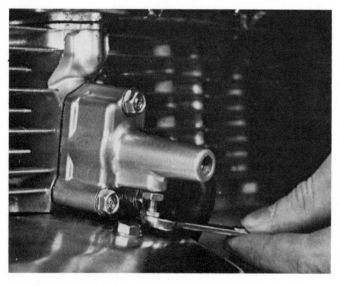

Below the chain tensioner on a Honda 750 is the locking bolt and nut.

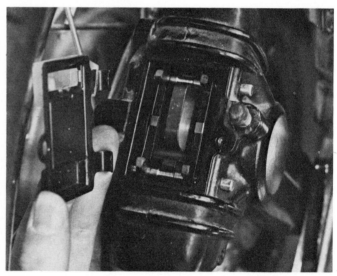

Some models have the brake pads covered in and this must be removed to check wear.

A caliper should not be split to change pads. Leave these bolts alone and remove the wheel.

Brake lining wear limit indicator on a rear drum brake, universal on modern machines.

Adjustment of the front brake is carried out by tightening this nut.

Do not forget to top up anti-freeze when servicing a water-cooled machine in winter.

Rear chain adjusters vary from model to model but the principle is the same.

Modern motorcycle batteries are generally reliable but need distilled water.

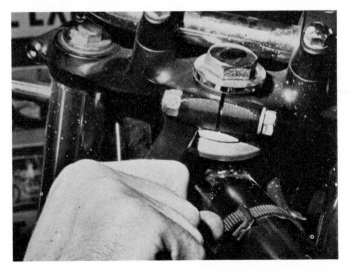

Head races should be adjusted if movement is felt in the forks. Do not overtighten.

A vital job if you enjoy life! Check the hydraulic brake fluid reservoir every week.

Service chart

	Two-stroke			Four-stroke		
	4000 miles	6000 miles	8000 miles	4000 miles	6000 miles	8000 miles
Transmission oil	R	R	R	R	R	R
Engine oil	T	T	T	T	R	T
Brake fluid	T	T	T	T	T	T
Coolant level	T	T	T	T	T	T
Battery	TC	TC	TC	TC	TC	TC
Spark plugs	R	CA	R	CA	CA	R
Contact points	CA	CA	R	CA	CA	R
Ignition timing	A	A	A	A	A	A
Contact cam felt	L	L	L	L	L	L
Carburettor	CA	CA	OCA	CA	CA	OCA
Oil pump	A	A	A			
Air filter	C		R	C		R
Control cables	LA	LA	LA	LA	LA	LA
Fuel filters	C		C	C		C
Tappets				A		A
Front fork oil	R		R	R		R
Steering head races	CA		CA	CA		CA
Tyres	IA	IA	IA	IA	IA	IA
Brake pads/shoes	CIA	IA	CIA	CIA	IA	CIA
Silencer de-carbonization	C		C			
Engine de-carbonization	C		C			
Drive chain and sprockets	LIA	LIA	LIA	LIA	LIA	LIA
Wheel spokes	IA		IA	IA	IG	IA
Swinging arm bushes	IG	IG	IG	IG	I	IG
Tacho, speedo, horn and lights	I	I	I	I		I
Oil filter				R		R

Key: R=Replace, T=Top up, I=Inspect, G=Grease, C=Clean, L=Lubricate, A=Adjust, O=Overhaul.

Engine Troubles

Identifying engine noise

The first sign that something is wrong with an engine is usually a change of note. Providing that you know how a healthy engine sounds, you can soon tell when all is not well. But locating the source of the offending noise is a more difficult task. Experience is essential when tracking down engine noise, so do not be afraid to get a second opinion from a dealer, or a knowledgeable friend.

The first clue to the source of the noise is the type of sound. If it is a very heavy thump or a deep rumble it is likely to be something large, such as the big-end bearing, especially if it seems to be coming from deep inside the engine. On a two-stroke [cycle] a light metallic rattle may only be due to a small amount of piston slap, which is quite acceptable on most two strokes, but it could be a worn small-end bearing.

The main task is to try and link the type of sound to a part of the engine that will cause that particular noise. As an example a rattle is more likely to be caused by a chain than a worn bearing. Tapping noises, on four-strokes, can generally be linked to valve gear or faulty camshafts.

The next clue in your search is the speed at which the noise occurs. If the thump, rattle or knock is directly related to the engine speed then start looking at the components running at engine speed such as big-ends, small-ends or the pistons. If the noise seems to be coming at half engine speed, then the valve gear is more likely to be suspect.

Road testing

You can find out quite a lot about an engine by road testing. If the problem noise is only apparent when the motor is pulling, and then only at low rpm, the ignition timing may well be suspect and could be jammed on full advance.

Pulling in the clutch and checking for noise will eliminate the gearbox as a possible cause, if the noise still persists. Also try the bike in all the gears. You may have an intermittent problem on the road caused by a faulty gear wheel.

An engine stethoscope is the ideal instrument for locating the not-so-obvious sounds. Alternatively, use a screwdriver against your ear, touching the blade end to the suspect area of the engine. It is best to use an insulated screwdriver if listening anywhere near the HT leads! If you do invest in an engine stethoscope listen to various healthy engines first, for it is surprising what awful noises are produced during the course of an engine's normal running. Once acquainted with normal engine noise a sick motor should be easy to identify.

Pinking [pinging]

A timing light can be useful to check the auto advance of an engine if you are having trouble with power loss or pinking [pinging] at the lower end of the power/rpm scale.

On multi-cylinder machines you can pull off one plug lead at a time to eventually isolate a faulty piston or a cylinder with low compression. A compression gauge can also be very useful. When using one you will get a better reading if the engine is hot and the throttle is held wide open. For this, the ignition should be disconnected.

If you have tried everything you can think of without success, you can, as a last resort, take your sick bike along to a dealer with electronic diagnostic equipment and have him sort it out for you.

Top: the obvious way to find out what is really wrong – road test the bike.

Below: Wear on a taper roller bearing can be spotted by examining the rollers for "polish" marks.

Substitution

This system is widely used by the trade to rectify a sick motor without actually finding out what is wrong with it. For example, if the symptoms seem to indicate a fault in the carburation then the whole carburettor is changed rather than taking the time to strip it down and locate the actual fault. Substituting parts is fine if you have the new parts to hand, but if you have to buy them it can get rather expensive, especially if you happen to guess wrongly.

With certain electrical items the only way you can check their efficiency under running conditions is to substitute a new component. Spark plugs are an excellent example of this. The substitution system of trouble tracing however, has limited value. Nobody is going to strip down an engine and fit a new big end just to see if the old one was worn after all.

Breakdown and misfires

Complete engine failure is probably the most annoying problem on the road but one of the easier faults to put right. Since the engine has stopped running something or other has definitely gone wrong and providing you follow a logical sequence of thought and checking, it should not be too hard to track down. Intermittent misfires (see below), on the other hand, are one of the hardest sources of trouble to locate. An engine that only plays up can be a real problem.

Breakdowns

The first thing to check after a breakdown is whether the fault is in the fuel line or the electrics. You should have had a fair indication of the cause of the fault by the way that the machine failed. If you had been travelling down the road at a modest 60mph and the engine instantly cut out, then there is a good chance that the ignition is at fault. Slowly reduced progress before the engine stops altogether is more likely a symptom of a fuel supply fault.

In the case of a total engine failure always remember that you need four things for the engine to run – fuel reaching the combustion chamber; air mixing with the fuel in the correct ratio; a good spark arriving at the correct time; and good compression in the cylinder. By remembering these four basics, and checking or eliminating them one at a time, you will find the fault.

Intermittent misfire

An intermittent fault is one of the hardest to track down simply because it is never there when you are looking for it. The first step in locating a fault of this type is to start with the basic service items – plugs, points, tappets, timing, (which are covered on pages 16 and 32). Only when satisfied that all are correct and that the engine has good compression should you proceed further. A large percentage of misfire problems are caused by poor servicing.

When tracking down a misfire you have to be a detective, collecting all the information that you can, examining all the clues and by a process of logical deduction arriving at the answer. Knowing your machine is vital. If, for example, you have a single-carburettor twin cylinder bike and the fault is an intermittent cutting out on one cylinder you can assume immediately that the fault is not in the carburettor since the one instrument feeds both of the cylinders. The same can apply to the contact breaker points, if one set triggers the coil for both cylinders. The ignition coil will feed both cylinders so is not likely to be faulty, but as it has separate HT leads one of these could well be at fault.

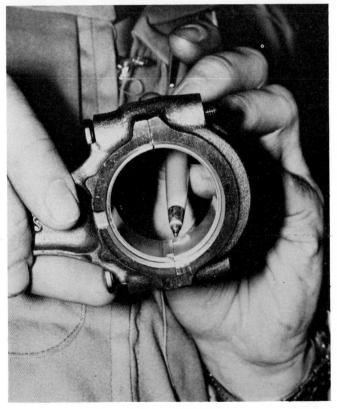

Top: When building up an engine a drop of oil on the bearing shells prevents a "dry" start.

Below: big end bearing shells are usually located like this.

51

Removing an engine

Taking an engine out of a bike usually looks more difficult than it actually is. But it is, however, also easy to make mistakes, especially when **you** are putting the engine back again.

Removal
The only real problems occur when a big, heavy engine is shoe-horned into a close-fitting chassis. The principles, however, are the same for all.

If the size of the motor is going to cause weight problems one way to reduce it and make the load a little lighter is to strip out the top end in place. Unless you have an engine stand this will make work on the engine easier.

It does not matter in which order you disconnect all the trimmings, except in cases where you have to remove one to get at the next. But if a shop manual is not available take a good look at the engine side covers, gear lever, kick-starts and so on. These pieces often have to be removed or they will foul the frame – and balancing a motor half in, half out, is no time to discover facts like this.

Other parts, like the spark plugs and coils, may not need to come out unless they protrude and are likely to become damaged. Next, drain off the oil in the engine and gearbox. Then loosen off parts that are likely to prove difficult to move, as this is more easily done while the engine is firmly held in place. Parts like sprocket retaining nuts are far easier to remove at this point.

Make a check list as each item is disconnected so that nothing is forgotten when you start to re-assemble. At the same time, note where spacers are fitted and which wires go where. Cables, electrical contacts and so on should be taped up by the seat where they will be out of the way.

Finally, have some strong pieces of wood at hand, so that as the engine mountings are disconnected you can support the engine weight by levering a length of wood between the frame tube and the underside of the engine. If you can take the weight off the mountings it will be easier to pull the bolts out.

Use the same method to line up the engine when ready to re-fit. Do not try and force the bolts through, but push a smaller rod, such as an old screwdriver, through and use this to make the holes line up. Get the biggest mounting bolt in this way and then the engine can be pivoted on it to line up the rest.

Before actually heaving the engine out of place, go round it carefully to ensure that everything is disconnected and that the odd earth connection or neutral indicator wire has not been forgotten. Most engines need tipping up and leaning to one side to manoeuvre them out of the frame. This process is usually a matter of trial and error. Before removing it, however, make certain that you have somewhere to put it.

Keep carefully to your check list when refitting the motor. It is easy to miss out little things like oil and ignition wires. Make sure everything has been connected up and tightened down; reset the timing; adjust the clutch, throttle, oil pump, chain and then try to start it. Should the motor run, let it warm up and then re-tighten all the nuts and bolts.

Check list	
Drain oil	Rear chain
Fuel lines	Oil pump cable
Exhausts	Oil lines (bleed pump)
Air slide/carbs	Adjust pump
Carb balance pipe	Wiring
HT leads/coils	Tachometer drive
Engine cover	Front mountings
Clutch cable/adjuster	Rear top mountings
Gear lever/brake pedal	Rear lower mountings and spacers

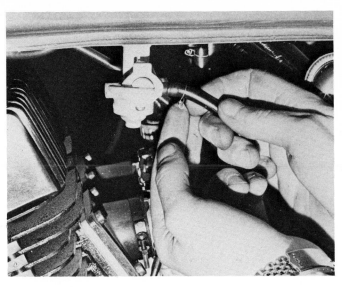

After draining the oil (four-strokes only) disconnect fuel lines and remove tank.

Remove alternator cover, using impact driver if necessary. Don't forget HT leads.

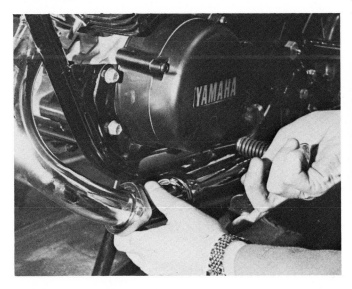

Exhaust pipe removal is simple, although rusted bolts can be difficult.

On the Yamaha 250 the clutch cable is held by a safety tag which has to be bent back.

Undo air cleaner hoses and push clear. Unscrew carburettor top and take out slides.

Take off oil pump cover, slacken cable adjuster and disconnect cable at the pump.

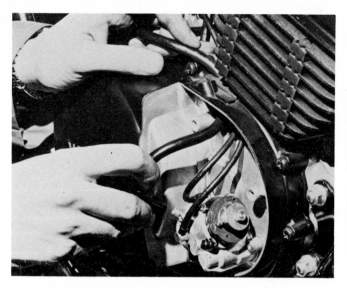

Disconnect the oil line from tank and either drain the tank or crimp the pipe.

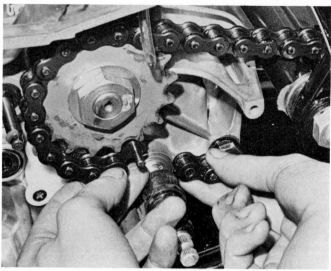

Disconnect chain if not needed to lock the engine to undo rotor or sprocket nuts.

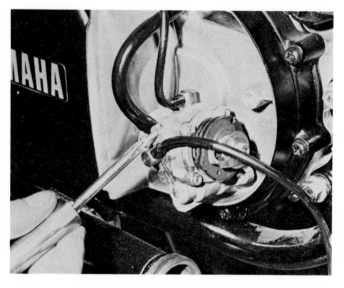

To bleed the pump, on rebuild, remove set screw in the body and turn plastic wheel.

Loosen front and rear engine mounts. Check that pedals etc. are not going to jam.

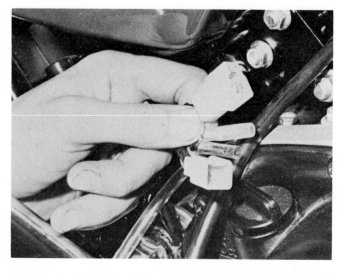

Disconnect wiring from the alternator. Label plug wires if necessary.

Strip out mounting plates and note where spacers are fitted. Lift out.

Carburettors

How they work

As the only link between an engine and the outside world, the carburettor has a major influence on the two things most riders would like to improve – performance and economy. It controls the amount of air getting into the engine and therefore governs its power output. It also meters the petrol [gas] mixing with the air, affecting fuel economy.

Carburettor tuning and balancing results in smooth running as well as maximum power from the smallest possible amount of fuel.

The basic carburettor

The simplest type of carburettor consists of a tube through which air is drawn into the engine by the displacement of the pistons. Because the air is moving, the pressure it exerts on the inside of the tube is less than that of the static air pressure on the outside. This pressure difference is used to draw fuel into the tube – a fuel line (at 'static' pressure) is led to a small hole in the side of the tube. At this fuel exit the pressure is lower, and fuel will flow through into the tube.

The fuel also needs to be broken up into tiny particles ('atomised') and spread evenly in the airflow to make a consistent mixture which will burn efficiently once it arrives inside the engine. This much can be achieved by slightly refining the tube/fuel line arrangement. The speed of the air depends upon the volume displaced by the pistons, the speed at which the motor is turning as well as the size of the tube. The first two are fixed for a particular motor, but the size of the tube can be altered to get optimum air 'speed' – for a given engine size and speed, a smaller tube gives a higher air speed. In many carburettors the tube is narrowed to speed up the air past the fuel orifice – this narrowing is called a venturi. The atomisation and distribution of the petrol can also be altered by changing the shape of the fuel orifice, usually by fitting a spray tube for the fuel to flow through.

The first snag is that while the size of the engine does not change much, its speed does alter considerably and so the gas speed will go up and down in proportion.

The problem with varying the gas speed is that if the air travels too slowly it will not break the fuel up into small enough drops and will not carry all the fuel into the engine. If it moves too quickly, friction between the walls of the tube and the air starts to be a problem.

One way around this is to put a valve in the venturi so that its size can be altered. On the fixed jet type of carburettor this valve is also used as a throttle which limits the amount of air allowed to pass through the carburettor into the engine. It is raised by opening the throttle control and is closed by the throttle return spring.

Total combustion

To get total combustion from fuel and air you need a mixture of 15 parts of air to 1 of petrol. Engines however, will run quite smoothly from ratios of less than 12:1 through to something like 18:1. Engines produce maximum power on a rich mixture (12 or 13:1) and maximum economy on a leaner mixture of about 18:1. Several problems arise as a result of an engine's ability to run on mixtures far from the ideal.

Running too lean makes the engine run hotter and eventually too lean a mixture will burn out pistons and valves.

Running too rich obviously wastes petrol but that is not all.

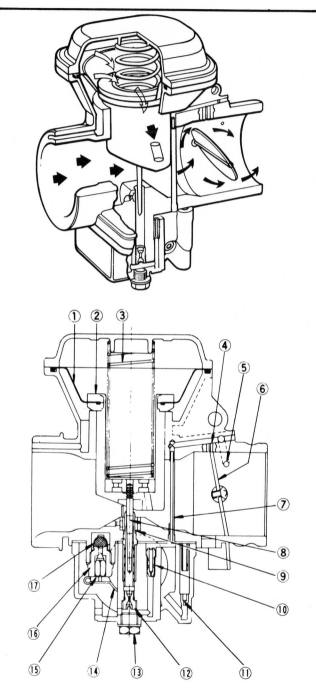

Constant velocity carburettor components and operation: the throttle valve controls air flow to the engine, governing speed and power. The depression in the intake passage is ducted above the piston valve, causing it to lift in proportion to the depression. This in turn lifts the needle to allow more fuel flow.
1 Diaphragm, 2 Piston valve, 3 Return spring,
4 Pilot by-pass, 5 Pilot outlet, 6 Throttle valve,
7 Pilot pipe, 8 Jet needle, 9 Needle jet, 10 Pilot jet,
11 Starter jet, 12 Main jet, 13 Drain plug, 14 Float
15 Needle valve, 16 Valve seat, 17 Fuel filter.

The unburnt fuel lines the cylinder walls and other areas where it prevents the oil from lubricating these places effectively. Hence the engine suffers from wear.

That is why the mixture strength has to be just right to suit the demands of the engine and if these change, the mixture strength has to be changed too.

Running conditions

Basically, there are four running conditions which the carburettor has to cope with: idling, part-throttle cruising, full-throttle acceleration and maximum speed.

At idle speed the throttle is closed and only a tiny bleed or by-pass allows air through into the engine. Some carburettors have an air jet to govern the airflow. These small proportions are beyond the scope of the main fuel system and the air bleed is directed over another small orifice, usually a simple drilling in the carburettor body, connected to the fuel supply. The fuel flows through the pilot jet which gives a coarse adjustment of the mixture strength. Fine adjustment is provided in the form of a tapered screw which regulates either the air flow or the fuel flow. When the twistgrip is slowly opened there is a stage where the pilot outlet cannot supply enough fuel yet the throttle valve is not open far enough for the main system to take over.

To avoid a 'flat spot' in this position a second pilot outlet, or pilot by-pass, is provided – the first outlet is on the engine side of the throttle valve, and the by-pass is on the far side so that it cannot supply fuel until the throttle is opened slightly. As the throttle is opened further the main system progressively takes over.

For idling, the engine only needs to produce enough power to keep itself turning, so tuning is a matter of making the mixture as weak as possible consistent with even running, without stalling when the throttle is opened.

At the other extreme, on full throttle, the engine needs maximum power while economy is a secondary consideration. The throttle valve is fully opened, the venturi is at a maximum and the fuel flow is governed by the main jet, the smaller of two jets screwed into the jet block immediately below the spray tube. Mixture strength is adjusted by changing the main jet for a larger or smaller one to make the mixture richer or leaner, respectively.

While full throttle acceleration requires immediate power, the engine will not be turning at maximum revs. To compensate for this, many carburettors have a device which temporarily richens the mixture when the throttle is snapped open. This varies from an 'accelerator' pump, which squirts fuel into the venturi as the throttle opens, to a reservoir of fuel under the spray tube which is sucked into the venturi by the sudden gulp of air. These methods are a bit imprecise, but as the engine conditions are rapidly changing anyway, they work well enough. No adjustment can usually be made here but even if it were possible, no amount of compensation would prevent the engine stalling below a particular speed, if the throttle is suddenly snapped open.

Cruising economy

Part-throttle cruising covers the widest range of running conditions and on a road bike, the positions in which the motor will spend most of its working life. Yet of all tuning operations this is probably the most neglected. The reason is simple, the motor will run with no sign of trouble on a wide range of mixtures and thus the rider has no immediate means of knowing whether he is wasting fuel or not. An erratic idle, on the other hand, is both obvious and annoying, while the risk of a blow-up on full power makes people pay more attention to main jet setting.

Part-throttle airflow is controlled by the throttle valve but if this reduces the venturi size, locally speeding up the air, there will be too much fuel drawn out into the airstream. So the fuel, already metered by the main jet, is passed through another jet (the needle jet) which obviously has to be larger in diameter than the main jet. To restrict fuel flow down to the right level (maximum economy needs a mixture approaching 18:1 rather than the 12:1 ratio given by the main jet) a tapered needle is fitted inside the needle jet. This is lifted, increasing the effective size of the jet, as the throttle valve is opened to allow more air through. At positions from roughly one-quarter to three-quarters full throttle, the size of the needle jet and the taper of the needle control the fuel flow. A fine adjustment can be made by raising or lowering the needle relative to the throttle. The needle is fixed by a spring clip which engages in a groove and by providing four or five such grooves the needle position can be altered. From three-quarter throttle to full throttle the main jet progressively takes over and the mixture is richened from the maximum economy setting to the maximum power setting.

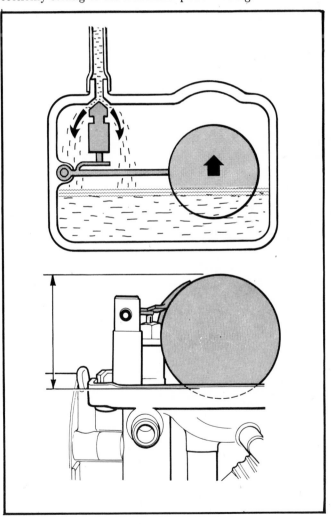

Float bowl operation (top) showing how the rising float shuts off supply. Float level is often measured from the flange to the bottom of the float and adjusted by bending the operating arm, making the valve shut at a higher or lower level.

At lower throttle openings, from idle to one-quarter throttle, the needle and needle jet still have an effect but this is offset to some extent by the shape of the throttle valave. This has a cutaway in the front edge (farthest from the engine) and the larger the cutaway the greater the airflow and the leaner the resulting mixture. None of the jets or other components completely dominates the settings for a particular throttle opening, though they each overlap. For example, changing the main jet will have greatest effect at full throttle, with lessening effects right down to half-throttle or possibly further.

The Float-chamber
There are two more items which affect the performance of the carburettor. The first is the float-chamber. If the jets were hooked up directly to the fuel tank, neat petrol [gas] could drain through them into the motor and the level of the fuel i.e. its pressure would be continually changing. The float chamber is arranged to supply the jets with a constant head of fuel, no matter what the level in the tank.

A fuel line supplies petrol [gas] into the chamber, which is built into the bottom of the carburettor or attached to the side of it, and inside the chamber there is a float which rises as the level of fuel rises. When the fuel reaches a certain height, the float shuts off a needle valve and prevents more fuel entering the bowl. As the engine uses up fuel, the level drops, the float drops, the valve opens and more petrol [gas] comes in.

The height at which the valve shuts off affects the mixture strength because the fuel has to be lifted through the jets into the venturi by the pressure drop in the airflow. The lower the level the farther the fuel has to be raised and the greater the force needed. So a low level tends to weaken the mixture all the way through the range, while a high level richens it. The level can be adjusted by bending the float mounting or the arm which operates the needle valve. On many carburettors this is done by measuring the distance between the bottom of the float and the face of the float chamber while the valve is held closed.

The choke
The second component is necessary for a temporary running condition – cold starting. Because the motor is turning slowly and because the fuel is cold and less volatile – less willing to be atomised – a rich mixture setting is necessary to make sure enough fuel reaches the cylinder for reasonable combustion. This can be done by restricting the air-flow by a choke or strangler or by incorporating a starter jet in the carburettor. When the choke is pushed 'on' it raises a jet to supply fuel into the intake in the same way that the other jet works. In the 'off' position the jet is lowered and does not operate.

The CV carburettor
Most of the above refers to fixed-jet carburettors. Another type widely used on motorcycles is the CV or constant velocity carburettor. The function of the float bowl, jets, needle and airslide is exactly the same as the fixed-jet type, the difference being that the airslide or piston valve is not linked to the throttle and a separate throttle valve (or butterfly valve) is used.

The piston valve is a close fit in the top body of the carburettor and the chamber above it is sealed either by a diaphragm or by piston rings around the valve itself. In the bottom of the valve a small hole opens into the venturi and the valve is held closely by a spring. As the throttle is opened with the engine running, the reduced pressure draws air out

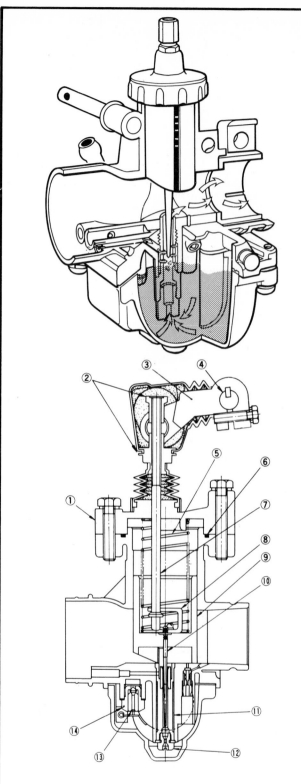

Fixed jet carburettor: in this type the throttle control lifts both the airslide (to flow more air) and the jet needle (to flow more fuel) in order to increase the fuel flow to the engine.
1 Carb top, 2 Throttle adjuster, 3 Throttle linkage arm, 4 Linkage shaft, 5 Return spring, 6 O-ring, 7 Throttle operating rod, 8 Jet needle set plate, 9 Throttle valve, 10 Jet needle, 11 Needle jet, 12 Mainjet, 13 Needle valve, 14 Valve seat.

of the chamber above the piston valve. The air under the diaphragm is at 'static' pressure and so the pressure below the diaphragm is greater than that above it – and the diaphragm, plus the piston valve, is lifted against the spring pressure. This also lifts the needle from the needle jet in the same way as the other type of carburettor.

More throttle allows more airflow, the speed under the piston valve increases, the pressure drops, so the valve is lifted further. This increases the size of the venturi, reducing the air speed back to its original level. In other words, the piston valve takes up a position where the pressures are balanced against the spring, the idea being to maintain a constant gas velocity through the venturi, hence the name.

The advantages of this system are that the constant velocity produces constant spraying and mixing of the fuel from the jets and that the piston valve opens an amount which corresponds not only to the throttle opening but also to the engine speed, thus the fuel metering can be made to match the demands of the engine more closely. The disadvantages are in a more complicated construction which obviously depends upon a good seal above the piston valve and the need for an extra valve which obstructs the air passage.

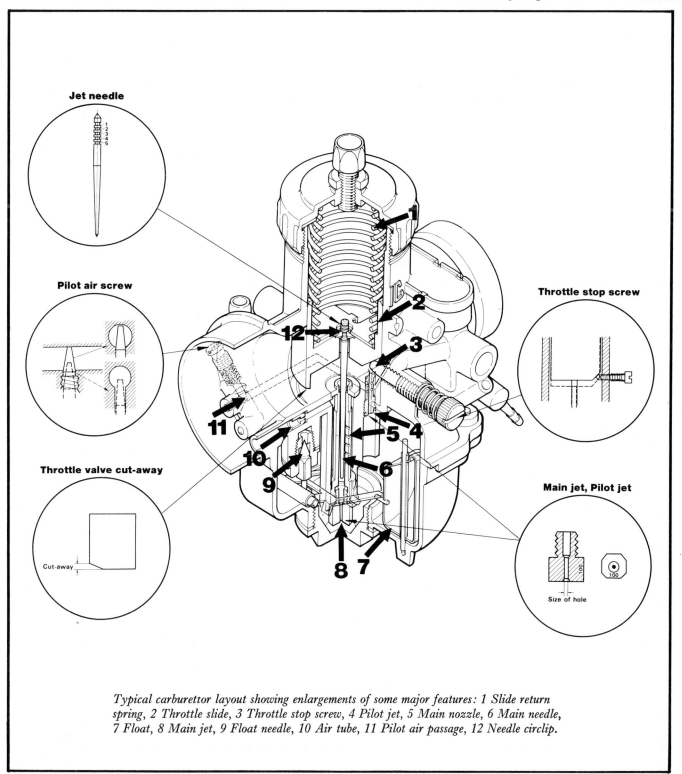

Typical carburettor layout showing enlargements of some major features: 1 Slide return spring, 2 Throttle slide, 3 Throttle stop screw, 4 Pilot jet, 5 Main nozzle, 6 Main needle, 7 Float, 8 Main jet, 9 Float needle, 10 Air tube, 11 Pilot air passage, 12 Needle circlip.

How to tune and balance

Carburettor tuning consists largely of compromising different characteristics to obtain an optimum blend of full power, easy starting, smooth running and economy. It is important that carburettors only be tuned after the rest of the engine has been checked over, properly adjusted and warmed up. For there is no point in refining the operation of the carburettor if other engine components are maladjusted.

When tuning, only make one change at a time to avoid balancing one alteration against another and upsetting the mixture range at a different engine speed.

After the motor has been properly serviced, the first thing to do is to check the air filter, as a clogged or dirty one will affect the mixture as much as any adjustment of the mixture screws. Next, take off the carburettor float chamber(s), clean out filters and the sludge traps in the bottom of the chamber(s) and check that the fuel lines are not obstructed or that there is an air lock in the tank.

Next reset the float height, checking that none of the float(s) is damaged. A punctured float can be identified by shaking the float and listening for petrol [gas] splashing around inside it. Also check that the needle valves are sealing. With just the weight of the float holding the valve closed you should not be able to blow through the fuel line.

Balancing

Where individual carburettors feed cylinders they can be regarded as completely separate units for tuning, but each carburettor must be balanced or synchronized with the others. This is simply to ensure that they all open together and by the same amount. After the correct settings have been reached, check that each carburettor is adjusted so that when the throttle is opened, each airslide lifts at the same moment. On full throttle each airslide should be out of sight at the top of the venturi, not sticking out into the venturi. Out of balance carburettors usually cause an uneven sound from the intake and engine vibration. Some types can be synchronised by removing a blanking screw from the side of the mixing chamber and opening the throttle until a pip on the airslide shows through the hole. The others should then be aligned similarly using the cable adjusters or throttle linkage.

When the engine is running the carburettors can be balanced by a check on the airflow into each one. It is possible to do this by holding a tube to the intake and listening, but the accuracy depends entirely on your experience and hearing. There are devices which push over the carburettor bellmouth and connect to a U-tube containing paraffin [kerosene] – any inequality in airflow between two carburettors is then shown by the unequal levels of fluid in the tube.

Going one stage further, a vacuum gauge will give a more precise reading and some carburettors have a blanked off stub which accepts an attachment for a vacuum gauge. On some CV types this is about the only way the carburettor can be balanced with any accuracy. A vacuum gauge can also be used to monitor carburettor tuning, particularly for getting maximum economy at cruising speeds. Because of the pulse flow, the gauge reading will not be steady, but this can be damped by using a fairly long flexible tube, bending it and putting a clamp on the bend to restrict it. A small screw clamp can be adjusted to give a steady reading at the gauge.

To balance the carburettors, an equal volume reading is needed on each one, which is done by adjusting the throttle stop or throttle linkage, at idle, and with the main control cable to the throttle slackened off. After balancing the carburettors use the main adjuster to take the slack out of the cable.

Tuning

The easiest way to tune carburettors is to follow a sequence which will let you see the maximum effect of any given adjustment and to make just one change at a time.

Idle speed is one of the easiest and the only one which will need repeating periodically. Slacken off the throttle cable, find the pilot mixture adjusting screw, which will be on the side of the carburettor body, and the throttle stop screw. This could either be on the side of the carburettor or the top or incorporated into the linkage. If you have the maker's settings (usually $1\frac{1}{4}$-$1\frac{1}{2}$ turns out from the fully home position) start with the mixture screw in this position. Then turn the throttle stop to slow the engine down until it falters. Next, turn the mixture screw whichever way is necessary to make the engine speed up. Bring it down again on the throttle stop. Carry on doing this until the idle speed is correct, with the engine running smoothly and responding properly when the throttle is slowly rolled open. Then re-adjust the cable.

Before adjusting the main jet check the spark-plug after a fast run. A great deal can be learned about the mixture by the colour of the spark plug. The insulator round the centre electrode should be tan or greyish-brown. A weak mixture makes the colour lighter and if it looks very light, white, shiny or blistered, the mixture is dangerously weak and the engine is probably running extremely hot.

A darker colour, even black and sooty, comes from rich mixtures. These will foul the spark plug. You can obtain peculiar results if you are using the wrong grade of spark plug; if you have wrong ignition timing, or if there is too much oil in a pre-mix two-stroke, etc., and that is another reason why the motor has to be in good adjustment before you start adjusting the carburettor(s).

What you are looking for, apart from the right plug colour, is smooth running; a good pick-up; no flat spots; no spitting in the carburettors or banging in the exhaust and no misfiring. The trouble is that all of these things can stem from other faults and, partly because the carburettors are easy to get at and tinker with, it is easy to jump to the wrong conclusions and create extra work.

The mid-range cruising and acceleration involves the operation of the airslide. As the throttle is progressively opened the pilot jet gives way to the effect of the airslide, via the pilot by-pass. After the quarter throttle mark the needle taper and the needle position have most effect, slowly being taken over by the needle jet and the main jet. In practice the airslide cutaway is the one which needs altering least often, and enough adjustment is usually available on the needle position alone.

While you have the pieces in your hand it is as well to check for wear: scuffing on the airslide or lateral play between the airslide and the carburettor body will allow air leaks. If the needle has any visible signs of scuffing or it is bent, it should be renewed. Wear in the needle jet is shown by an oval hole – when it reaches the stage of being noticeable the jet should be scrapped.

Brakes, Chassis and Wheels

Handling

Handling faults are many and varied, often setting up a complex chain of reactions from what is basically a very simple source – such as a soft tyre or a worn head bearing. Usually the problem is in identifying the fault, which is not an easy thing to do if it takes the form of leaps and lurches at 70 mph.

Also, many symptoms of poor handling are related to the rider and the road surface. There are many examples of this – possibly the most dramatic being the rain-groove concrete sections found on some motorways. The rippled concrete makes some machines feel as if both tyres have gone flat and curiously it has a much greater effect on good-handling bikes. This in turn seems to indicate that machines with mediocre handling are this way because of flexibility in the wheels, forks and frame. As the wheels try to track along the concrete grooves, this flexibility allows the wheels some freedom without transmitting the alarming feedback to the rider.

The rider
The rider himself can amplify or minimise poor handling qualities. It has been found that changing the riding position can radically change the fine compromise between comfort and good handling and that steering techniques make a difference to the way a bike feels. It is impossible to say how much of this is psychological – but as long as the rider is happy that is what really counts. On most light machines with good handling you 'think' the bike through turns and if asked exactly where you applied the force to make the machine bank over, you would have problems in describing precisely what you did. Eventually you might come up with the explanation that you steered with your knees – but ride along and push your right knee into the tank as hard as you like and nothing will happen. A closer examination will reveal that you bend slightly at the hips and steer very lightly right – to turn left. The centrifugal reaction and the gyroscopic precession of the front wheel, produced by a light, right-steering effort causes the bike to bank left, and the forces involved are very small.

The same technique on a big, heavy bike feels terrible. At low speeds it will lurch and try to fall into the bend – at high speeds it will be hard to keep it on a precise line and it may start a long, rolling weave. Such bikes respond much more predictably to being steered on the handlebars. To turn left you make a positive, conscious effort to turn the bars right, you keep up the pull on the bars all the time you are in the corner and balance the considerable left-banking force with power. Suddenly a heavy bike loses its sloppy feel and responds much more precisely.

These kinds of quirks (rather than faults) happen on bikes which are in perfectly good condition. A fault will show up as a change in the way the bike behaves under certain conditions. There are, however, many things you can do to improve poor handling, even when it is a design fault.

First handling and road holding should be distinguished. Handling is the way the bike feels and responds, roadholding is the way it unsticks. You could measure the first by how easily the bike frightens you and the second by how frequently you fall off.

Pitching or bouncing
Pitching or bouncing is the bike moving up and down on its suspension. If it happens in a straight line it is probably a

Top: Legal minimum tyre tread depth in the UK is 1mm but weaving is worsened at around 3mm. Pressures also affect handling.

Bottom: Changing riding position and the type of handlebars can make a big difference to handling characteristics. Moving the rider's weight forward may cure weaving.

fault of the suspension. One way – the traditional way of improving handling – is to stiffen the springs. This does not actually cure anything, it just moves the problem elsewhere. The bike may become more stable – the harder springs will reduce wheel movement – but bumps will then tend to lift the whole machine and it will give a less comfortable ride. Also the suspension will not let the wheels follow the ground so closely and ultimately performance will suffer – it is not just a whim of fashion that racers now have upwards of seven inches of wheel movement. The real answer is to control the wheel movement which may mean experimenting with different grades of oil in the forks or using better rear shock absorbers than the original equipment.

If the pitching happens in corners, it may still be a suspension problem but because of the nature of motorcycle steering, plus the fact that the bike is banked over it will not appear as pure pitching. As the bike lifts up and down the cornering forces change and it will weave or yaw. The bars may oscillate from side to side as if the front wheel was following a series of S-curves, or the steering head may nod from side to side without any appreciable movement from the bars. In either case the oscillation may be gentle and slow or it may be rapid. It seems that the causes can be the same, the different effects on different machines being related to the amount of damping (or resistance to weaving) and the stiffness the chassis has in different planes.

Weaving

Weaving, unfortunately, can come from many sources. Recent research has established that any castoring wheel, whether it is on a tea trolley or motorcycle, will go unstable at a certain speed. The speed at which this happens depends on several design factors: castor angle, trail, axle load and the difference in inertia between the top of the forks and the bottom of the forks, are the main ones. There are also secondary effects from the flexibility of the wheels, forks and frame, from the tyres and from the machine's centre of gravity or the way the bike is loaded.

The front wheel is the one which gets most attention as it has the obvious castoring construction, and it is where the symptoms of steering problems show up. However, the rear wheel is also castoring; it too pivots on the steering axis and its trail equals the bike's wheelbase plus the trail of the front wheel. There is no point in looking for perfection; a wheel which goes unstable at 120 mph is perfectly all right on a machine which cannot exceed 100 mph, but most bikes are a bit closer to the edge than this and a slight fault can take them into the danger area. A wheel which goes unstable at 90 mph is unsuitable on a machine which is capable of travelling more than 100 mph.

As weaving in one form or another makes up the majority of handling faults and as it can originate from so many areas, it helps if you can narrow down the field to different types of weaving.

Handlebar wobble

The simplest form of weave is handlebar wobble along a straight, smooth road. This usually happens at definite speeds either around 40 mph or 80 mph. It is usually a classic case of wheel instability – a design fault – and when it is a feeble wobble, only building up if you provoke it, it can be checked or damped out by fairly minor alterations. It could be caused – or made worse – by fitting a tail load such as a rear carrier; by overtightened head bearings or some similar restriction;

by additional weight on the handlebars, such as a fairing; or by fitting tyres which are not compatible with the machine. Some off-road bikes weave badly at top speed – this is simply because of their steering geometry, and is the price you pay for having ultra-quick steering at low speeds.

If the weave shows up immediately after you have completed work on the machine, the cause and cure should be obvious. Otherwise the best cure seems to be to move weight forward by changing the riding position, fitting lower, narrower bars etc. Experiments with rear suspension position, giving a different ride height, tyre pressures (or even types of tyre if you can afford it) may also push the instability speed above the limits of the bike. A good, frame-mounted fairing which carries the headlamp, should improve things, while a handlebar mounted fairing might make things worse.

Cornering

Weaving and pitching in turns (usually at high speed) or after the bike hits a bump, means that the chief suspect has to be flexibility in the chassis or some suspension defect. Check that the tyre pressures are as recommended or a few pounds per square inch higher – ideally front and rear should not differ by more than 3 psi and the tyres should be true on the rims.

Check that axle clamps are correctly fitted and that any fork brace is left in place

Check that the shock absorbers do work; it should be easy to compress the suspension and the shocks should take over on the rebound, making the bike return to its static position more slowly than when the springs were squashed.

Feel for any play in the front forks, wheel bearings and steering head. With the bike supported so that the wheel is off the ground, the only movement discernible should be the rotation of the wheel and the smooth pivoting of the forks about the steering head.

Look for loose spokes in both wheels and feel for any play in the swing-arm bearing. With the wheel clear of the ground, holding the frame in one hand and the rear of the wheel in the other, you should not be able to move the wheel in a sideways direction.

While you are checking the wheels make sure everything is screwed up tight, including the mudguard stays, and that axle clamps are correctly fitted. Most have a right and wrong way round and some have to be tightened evenly while others are fitted to leave a gap at the rear of the fork leg. If this does not eliminate the trouble, look for run-out in wheel spindles, swing-arm spindles, steering head stem or a cracked frame.

This sort of problem could well be tyres or rear shock absorbers which do not do their job properly and short of the expense of trying new ones the only answer is to seek out someone who has had a similar experience and cured it.

Low speed weaving

Weaving at very low speeds, or a tendency for the bike to fall into a turn, the bars swinging violently with the machine, is usually a feature of heavy bikes. It is made much worse if the front tyre is too soft or if the head bearings are too tight. A tight wiring harness can restrict steering movement enough to cause this problem and a fairing mounting which chafes on the fork yoke can make a bike almost unrideable below 20 mph.

Twitching

Twitching, a very rapid but short-lived weave, happens when bikes cross raised lines or ridges in the road, hitting them at a shallow angle. This starts to happen when the tyres wear or if they are run at the wrong pressures.

Other kinds of weaving happen under acceleration or braking, sometimes because the machine is simply too powerful for its chassis. Once again it is a matter of checking out play in wheels and suspension, making sure that hydraulic calipers are not sticking and checking tyres for pressure and truth. It may be worth making 'timing' marks on the tyre and rim to show up any tyre creep, which would eventually rip the valve out of the tube. If there is any creep fit a security bolt.

Quite often there is no clearly defined weave or wobble but the bike just feels insecure when you put it into a turn, like riding on a wet surface. This, unfortunately is just the way some bikes are and any improvement has to be a matter of experiment.

You can experiment with rear shock absorber pre-loads, even different springs or different units; or you can try the bike with higher tyre pressures (treat 25 psi as an absolute minimum) and with different grades of oil in the front forks. You can alter the riding position – which often has surprising results. Some machines lend themselves to having bracing pieces fitted. A tube can be fitted over engine mounting bolts where the bolt is forcing the frame tubes to be sprung – the tube acts as a spacer and gives the bolt something solid to tighten against.

If the machine pulls to one side, or has abnormally heavy

Prolonged series of bends are great for the rider – if his machine is handling properly.

steering the wheel alignment is likely to be wrong, either through bad adjustment or a bent frame or forks.

Slightly bent forks after a crash may not be apparent until they are disassembled, but can have a drastic effect on the steering, as well as affecting the suspension movement. Pulling to one side on acceleration or braking has to be a deflection in the suspension putting the wheels out of line as the springs move.

Juddering

The remaining handling symptom is juddering, pattering or vibration through the handlebars, which comes from one or other of the wheels. It could be caused by the wheel not being balanced or more likely by run-out on the tyre or rim. You can check this roughly by having a pointer fixed against a fork leg just touching the tyre or rim and turning the wheel – you'll see any run-out. Small amounts can be corrected by deflating the tyre and thumping it back centrally, or, if it is the rim, by tightening and loosening spokes a little 'at a time to pull the rim back into line.

Loose or broken spokes can also produce wheel pattering – by the time you feel it the problem will be serious and the wheel should be attended to immediately as in that state it could collapse altogether.

Run-out or ovality on brakes and worn wheel bearings can also make the bike judder and shake and with these problems it is serious structural areas that are at fault. You can play about with shocks, springs and riding positions with a fair amount of impunity. Spoke failures, steering restrictions and grabbing brakes are of a much more serious nature. Check them over, but if there is any doubt, or if a weave suddenly appears which you cannot trace, do not just leave it. You may be worrying about nothing, but it does not cost anything to have a dealer tell you so.

Top: In fork bushes you can see or feel play by using any sort of lever.

Bottom: Head bearings which are too tight or too loose can cause steering problems.

Changing and balancing

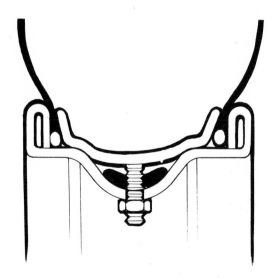

Deflate the tyre and remove any security bolts fitted to the wheel rim.

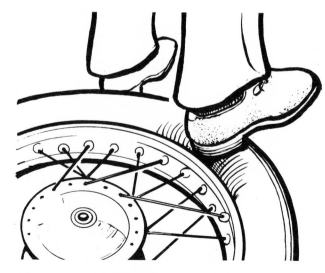

Break the seal which the beaded edge of the tyre will have formed against the rim.

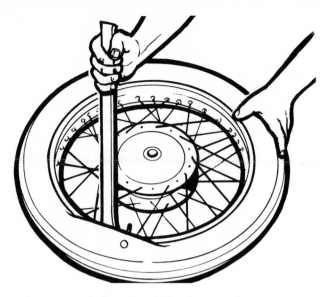

Use a lever to work the edge of the tyre over the rim, starting near the valve.

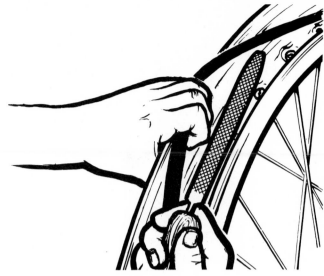

To remove tyre, repeat process on other side. File spokes which protrude above nut.

Use two levers to work tyre off, keeping opposite side pushed right into the rim well.

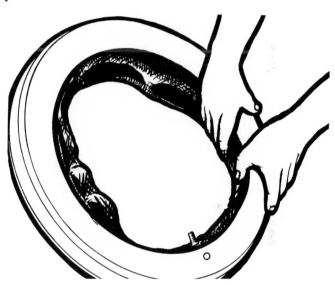

To refit, push one bead into the rim and feed the tube into place.

When one side is off, the valve locknut can be undone and the tube removed.

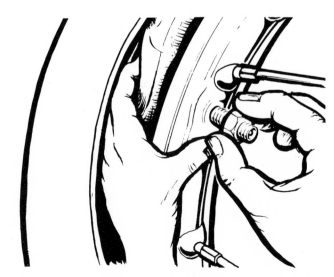

Fit the valve and locknut loosely, slightly inflate tube and check its fitting.

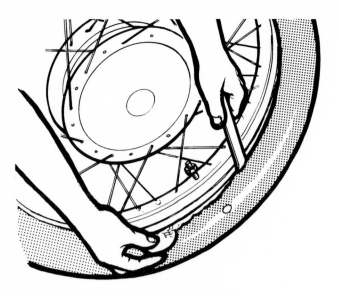

Ease the lip of the tyre over the rim – lubricate it with liquid soap.

Inflate tyre, thumping if necessary, to make it sit true on the rim.

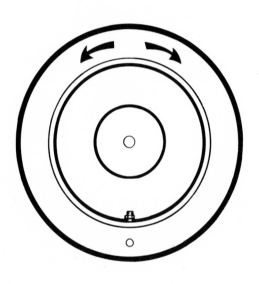

Fit the second bead of the tyre, starting opposite the valve and working round.

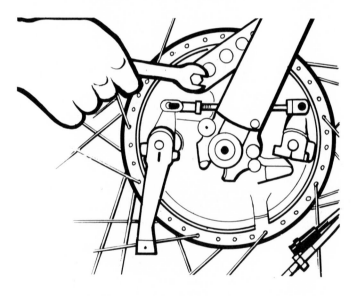

When refitting wheel, ensure speedo drive dog engages and check tightness of all bolts.

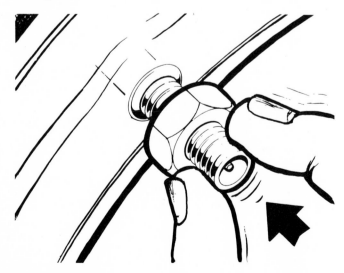

Make sure tube does not get trapped or twisted and that valve seats squarely.

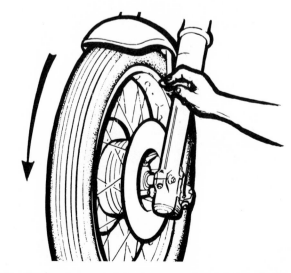

Spin the wheel and use a pointer to ensure that it is true between the forks.

Brake trouble

A variety of types of brake are fitted to modern machines. These include cable and hydraulically operated discs, drum brakes and even hydraulic cone brakes. The procedure for fault finding however is basically the same for all types.

Basic checks
Starting with the hydraulics, be sure to use a fluid of the recommended specification, or you will run into problems with the fluid boiling and the brakes going spongey. In extreme cases the wrong choice of fluid may well attack the rubber seals and you will lose your brakes altogether.

The flexible hose that carries the fluid to the caliper should be checked for any signs of chafing or twisting into a position where it may be trapped, as the suspension compresses under heavy braking.

Topping up the brake fluid from time to time will be necessary, as the pads wear down. Constant topping up, however, indicates a fluid leak and this will have to be located and corrected before the slow leak turns into a burst seal or a split hose. Leaking seals can be replaced, but check for scored or damaged cylinders; for re-rubbering these would be a waste of time and money.

Cables, at one time restricted to drum brakes only, are now also found on some bikes with disc brakes. Cables tend to stretch for the early part of their life and then settle down. So on a new bike or bike with a newly fitted cable check the cable regularly for stretch. Make sure that you check the inner cable near the lever for any signs of chafing or the nipple pulling away from the end. A good clean route from lever to brake will extend the life of the cable; it if follows a tortuous path, then the loads on it will be increased, as well as making it heavier in operation.

Modern cables are nylon lined but this does not mean that they do not need lubrication from time to time. Rain still tends to find its way inside the cable and the inner portion rusts. A decent grease gun device is the only sure way of lubricating the entire length of the inner cable.

Most rear drum brakes are operated by a rod and there is not too much that can go wrong here. The main points to watch are poorly fitted, or missing, split pins and loose adjusting nuts. Grease these periodically on the adjuster thread. If there is no locknut on the rear brake rod then there should be a spring which bears on the adjuster and stops it unwinding – make sure that it is not missing.

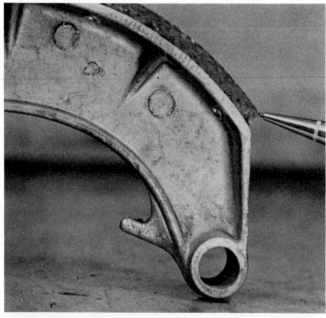

Top and bottom left: sharp edges on the brake linings are to be avoided, even on the trailing edges. The answer is to ease the edges down with a coarse file.

Above top: rod type operated rear brake. Ensure spring is replaced after stripping.

Above: what a brake lining should look like and, right, one impregnated with oil and ready for replacement.

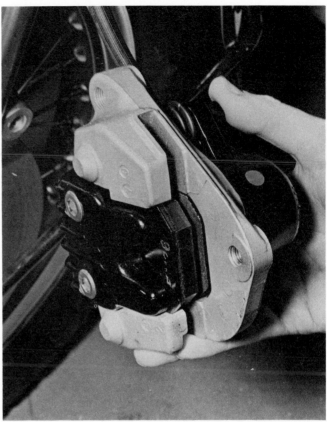

Symptoms of faulty brakes: juddering

On a disc brake the main cause of judder is disc run-out. This can be checked by using a dial gauge against the edge of the disc. Different makers give different tolerances for their bikes so you will have to check that your brake disc is within the original limits as set out by the particular manufacturer. If the run-out exceeds the limits then buy a replacement disc.

If the disc should vary in thickness this will cause a judder that will not show up as run-out on the dial gauge. Again makers give tolerances for the thickness of their disc units and the disc should be renewed if the thickness is below the maker's specifications.

If you suspect run-out or thickness variation and you do not have access to a dial gauge you will have to have it checked by a dealer.

Scoring of the disc does not have such a pronounced effect on the braking efficiency but it does reduce pad life considerably, so a badly scored disc should be renewed. This will save money in the long term.

Judder from a drum brake is usually an indication that the drum is oval. Provided that it is not too severe, the drum can be re-machined to correct this and new, oversize, linings fitted. The same cure can be applied in the case of a badly scored drum.

A point to look out for, before replacing discs or having drums skinned, is that wheel bearings in poor condition can give the same effect as disc run out or drum ovality. This is because the drum or disc is only held rigid to the wheel, so if the wheel runs out, due to worn bearings, so will the disc or drum.

Another source of trouble from the wheel bearing area is grease from the bearings finding its way into the drum or onto the disc. Greased brake linings may prolong the life of the drum but they certainly will not help brake efficiency. Make sure that the seals in the hubs are in good condition and always renew them if fitting new bearings.

Left: single disc brake with chromium plated or stainless steel disc. The caliper is mounted in front of the leg.

Right: some manufacturers have found that handling is improved by mounting the caliper behind the fork leg, as here.

Holding brakes

Brakes that work without being operated can be dangerous and should be corrected at the first sign of this. 'Holding on' with a disc brake can be caused by a fault in the hydraulics, such as overfilling of the master cylinder, or by a mechanical fault.

A common fault with single piston calipers is that the caliper does not move freely on the holding shaft. This means that after the brake has been applied and the static pad pulled across onto the disc, it remains there, rubbing against the brake disc at all times. This brings about two problems: first, the bike is slowed down due to the braking effect and secondly the pads glaze up. The answer is to remove the caliper and free it off then remove the pads and clean them with emery cloth. Glazed brake pads can be cured in the same way as glazed linings by rubbing them with abrasive cloth.

A drum brake that holds on could be due to simple over adjustment of the cable. If the adjustment is too tight then the shoes will start to contact with the drum, as they expand when the brake is applied.

Operating cams seizing can also cause the brake to hold on. This can be prevented by greasing the pivots with a high melting point grease. You must use an HMP grease, normal grease will melt as the brake heats up and run onto the linings.

If a drum brake grabs with only light application of the brake lever, it is possible that the leading edge of the lining needs chamfering down. If there is a twin leading shoe then both linings will have to be done. The idea is to provide a progressive action to the lining application, and prevent over-braking.

The disc brake that will not self centre is not so much of a problem. If the static pad is holding against the disc and you cannot cure it by freeing off the caliper, it may only be the brake pipe that is holding the caliper to one side. This may have become bent after a fall, or by damaging the caliper when changing pads. The repair is quite simple: first apply the brake and then put a 'set' in the brake pipe. This will neutralise the pipe and ensure that the caliper remains central after you release the brake.

Brake modification

There are many pitfalls to trap the unwary when it comes to improving the performance of a machine's braking system. Fitting harder linings to an otherwise standard drum brake for example. Frequently the result of this modification is to greatly increase lever pressure and reduce the braking efficiency at lower operating temperatures. Harder linings only improve braking at higher temperatures, such as you find under racing conditions.

Another favourite 'modification' is to fit air scoops. This has a two-fold effect. The first is to blow cold air over the linings, which may already be running too cold, the second is to scoop road dirt into the brake. If you must fit air scoops on a road machine, make sure that the intakes are covered with a gauze filter of some description to keep out the dirt. Air scooped into the front of the bike needs an exit at the rear, so do not forget to fit an exit scoop.

An effective way to improve braking is to fit an additional disc. Some large capacity machines can be fitted with a twin front disc, but you must change the master cylinder at the same time to keep the leverage ratios correct.

Until recently it was believed that changing a stainless steel or chrome disc for a cast-iron one helped wet weather braking. Later tests have indicated that the improvement is minimal.

In Britain research laboratories have found that it is brake pads which are most crucial to performance. Current experiments have embraced slotted discs which produce a marginal improvement, but the most vital findings have occurred with slotted pads. Here, wet weather braking has been substantially bettered.

It is not advised that owners modify existing pads themselves, as depth of slot is critical if the unit is not to break up during use.

A cable operated rear drum brake. The spring plays a crucial part.

Check the hydraulic fluid line to the rear disc brakes regularly.

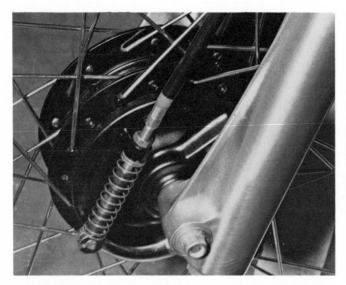

Full width drum brake of a type commonly found on low capacity roadsters.

Typical lightweight trail bike front brake. Normally efficient and simple to overhaul.

Electrical Systems

Electrical fault finding

Despite the complexity of motorcycle wiring diagrams the majority of circuits can be broken down into quite simple units. The source of power – usually a battery – feeds along a line to the load – e.g. a light bulb – and the power returns via an earth which is usually a connection to the machine's frame. Along the line there will be a fuse, switches and various connectors. A simple failure, such as a blown bulb, is equally simple to cure, but it is worth the price of the bulb to find out why it went in the first place. A blackened bulb glass or a filament burnt in the centre indicates voltage surge or old age. If the filament is broken at the end but the small weld is intact, the cause is likely to be vibration. The easiest cure for the latter is to remount the light unit on rubber pads or rubber grommets, making sure it has a good earth connection.

Voltage surge can be caused by poor connections, particularly a corroded earth connector. On direct lighting machines it can also happen if the dip-switch is a bit 'sleepy' in switching from high to low beam. It may also be caused by the 'normal' output of the generator being a little high, in which case the best cure is to fit a clipper diode in parallel with the light or as a last resort, a 12V bulb in a 6V system.

Other failures are more difficult to trace and the best way to pinpoint the fault is by testing for continuity. You can do this with a voltmeter, test lamp, or an ohm-meter. If the fault is a short circuit, blown fuse or charred wiring, it is better to disconnect the bike's battery before you damage it. You can still hook it up to the meter to test individual components. Basically, when using a voltmeter, the job is a matter of trying each part of the circuit in turn until you reach a point where you do not get a reading – and the fault lies in that section. You do exactly the same thing with an ohm-meter except that this is independent of the battery and where there is continuity it reads zero, reading infinity for an open circuit. It also has the advantage that you can check earth connections – a voltmeter can only be used if there is a load in the circuit and then only up to the load.

The generator

Motorcycles use quite an array of generators ranging from powerful 3-phase alternators, to a simple coil which is merely held near a rotating magnet. They have one thing in common – either one, three or six coils are connected, in various patterns, to provide the output. Each of these coils must be unbroken, so a continuity test across any two of the output leads must be positive, although the ohm-meter will read a low resistance value instead of zero. If a coil has broken you will get an open circuit reading and, unless the break is in the external connections, you cannot mend it, so all you need to do is replace it. Having disconnected the output leads, the generator should be insulated from earth; there should be open circuit between any one of the leads and the engine. If not, the insulation on the coils has broken down.

A partial break is not so easy to spot without full test data from the manufacturer's shop manual but if you are not getting full battery voltage at the battery and the regulator and rectifier are working, the battery and connections are healthy, then the generator is the only possible cause.

Three-phase alternators and DC generators have a further refinement, a field coil which replaces the permanent magnet.

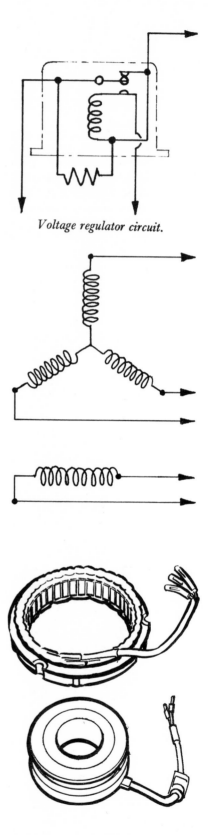

Voltage regulator circuit.

Alternator components (rotor and stator) and – above – connections for a three-phase alternator, energised by a separate field coil.

This should have continuity and should not be earthing, except through one of its connecting leads. You should inspect and check for continuity the brushes or slip rings through which power is supplied to the moving coil. When the battery is partially discharged, full battery voltage is supplied to the field coil.

The rectifier

The rectifier is a series of diodes which will only pass electric current in one direction, connected so that they convert alternating current to direct current in order to charge the battery. There may be four diodes, in which case there will be two input connections from the alternator, or there may be six diodes with three input leads from the alternator. In both cases there will be two output connections which supply the battery, one of which will be earthed, possibly through the rectifier's mounting bolt. To test the rectifier you need an ohm-meter or a test lamp and battery, and you test for continuity in opposite directions. Connect one test lead to any of the input connectors and the other test lead to each of the output connectors in turn; note whether it shows continuity (bright light or low to zero ohm reading). Reverse the test leads and repeat the test. There should be continuity in one direction and open circuit or at least a very high resistance in the opposite direction. Repeat the test for each of the input connectors. The rectifier is faulty (and will need replacing) if any of the tests produces continuity in both directions or open circuit in both directions.

The regulator

The regulator controls the current reaching the field coil, increasing or reducing the generator's output to suit the state of the charge of the battery. The battery must be in good condition before the regulator can be tested. Again, the manufacturer's test data is needed for a full test. Basically, however, you connect an ammeter in the lead to the field coil and a voltmeter across the battery connection and ground. Running the engine, the field current should be about $2\frac{1}{2}$ amps, if the voltage is less than 13V; and as the voltage increases the current should be cut to just over 1 amp at 13.5 to 14.5 volts, and zero to 1 amp as the voltage nears 15V. The voltage should not exceed 15V at any time.

The field current is altered by a solenoid which moves a double-faced contact breaker. In its first position it supplies battery voltage straight to the field coil. As the points open the battery is connected to the field coil via a resistor and then on making contact on the opposite face the field coil is effectively shorted out. Some adjustment is possible by altering the points gap. One point will normally have an adjusting screw, while bending the arm gives adjustment on the other. If the field current is excessively high, or if there is not continuity through to the field coil in the first two positions the regulator or field coil is faulty.

The battery

Most electrical faults stem from the battery, either as it wears out and runs flat or overcharges. Before starting any other electrical checks, test the battery condition and connections. The electrolyte level should be between the max and min marks, or if there are no marks, should cover the internal plates. If it is low, top it up with distilled water. Look to see if the electrolyte is clear – if it is cloudy or has sediment on the bottom, the plates in one of the cells may be breaking up and shorting through the sediment. The plates should be

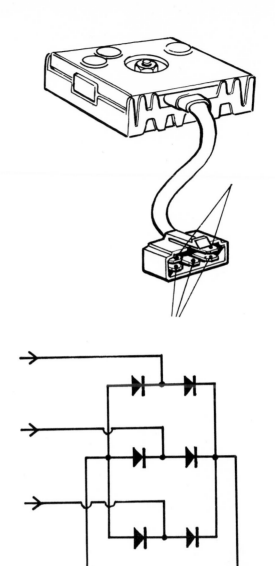

Rectifier for a three-phase AC input. The six diodes route the alternating current to give DC at the two output connections.

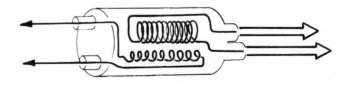

Construction of an ignition coil arranged to fire two spark plugs together (large arrows). The primary winding is connected to the battery and the contact breakers.

clean and not buckled, a deposit on them means that they have started to sulphate, effectively reducing the battery's capacity. Finally, clean any corrosion off the terminals and make sure there is metal to metal contact. Also, check that the breather tube is not trapped or blocked.

The only way to determine a battery's state of charge is by checking the specific gravity of each cell with a hydrometer. The specific gravity should not vary from cell to cell and for a fully charged battery it will be 1.26 to 1.28 depending on the temperature. As the battery is discharged, the specific gravity will fall. As a rough check, a good battery will light a headlamp bulb brightly and keep it bright for several minutes. If the battery is discharged or faulty the light will quickly go dim. Batteries should always be charged at the slowest possible rate – say $\frac{1}{2}$ amp to 1 amp – and should be charged about once a month if the machine is stored. If not the s.g. will fall and the plates will start to sulphate, or in cold weather the electrolyte may freeze as the freezing point is raised when the s.g. falls.

The ignition coil
The simplest way to test an ignition coil – and the whole circuit – is to remove a plug, rest it on the cylinder head with the HT lead connected and turn the engine over. A clear spark should be visible at the plug. If it is not, hold the bare end of the HT lead close to the head and repeat the test. If this sparks, the plug is faulty.

The coil actually has two coils, one called the primary which carries battery voltage, and the other, the secondary, in which the high spark-plug voltage is induced. If a faulty coil is suspected, check that power is reaching the coil from the ignition switch and that there is continuity between the two primary terminals. There are various wiring arrangements on different types of coil and depending on these the secondary winding should have continuity from the plug terminal to the contact breaker terminal, to the second HT (plug) terminal or, to earth. Ignition faults can be caused by poor HT wiring, dirty contact points or a faulty capacitor. The first two can be checked visually; the capacitor by substitution. Sometimes merely disconnecting the capacitor while the engine is running will show if it is faulty – if it is, there will be no change in the symptoms. If it is healthy there will be severe arcing at the contact breaker points and the engine will probably misfire. Because it is possible for wiring to break inside apparently healthy insulation, carefully check for continuity all through the system.

Using a stroboscope to set timing by a light flashing each time the ignition fires.

A strobe light "freezes" moving parts so that alignment of timing marks can be seen.

Lighting

Lighting problems can be many and various, yet while some of the problems are the same, the solutions can be different according to the circumstances.

For example, a machine with a 6-volt alternator can have its lighting improved in several ways depending on the owner's requirements. Conversion to 12-volts with a heavy duty alternator and a more powerful headlight would be the ideal solution. But a simpler alternative would be to fit an extra spot lamp to the existing system, particularly if it were only needed for short periods of around 20 minutes at a stretch. (Used over longer periods it would drain the battery). This solution would be cheaper and involve less work.

Better lights

Better lights can be gained in two ways: either by fitting a light unit or bulb with a greater wattage; or by fitting a more efficient light unit, for example a quartz halogen unit, which gives more light for the same amount of electrical power.

Several problems can ensue fitting better lights. In the first case a greater wattage may stretch the electrical system too far and there will not be enough left to keep the battery charged. This particularly applies when an additional light is fitted and the result is that the battery gradually runs down. However, this takes time and overloading the system may pay off if you want a spotlight but do not intend to use it for long periods.

Machines with a three-phase alternator (putting out in excess of 150W) can usually stand extra lighting quite comfortably but these machines usually have adequate lights anyway. Kawasakis with their standard 45/40W headlamps are one exception. Probably the best all-round solution is to fit a new light unit, such as a sealed beam unit, which fits easily and is relatively cheap.

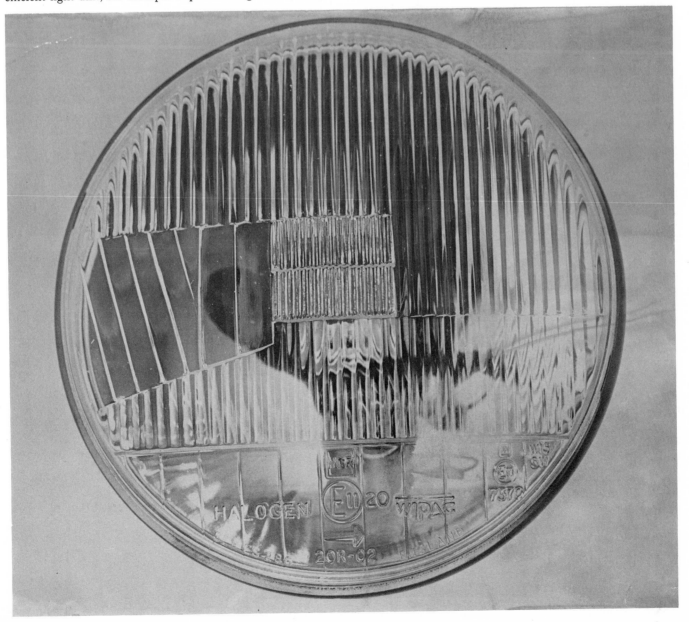

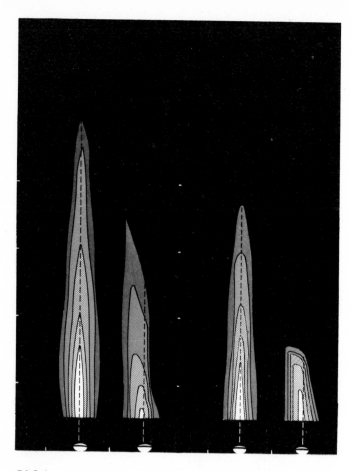

Lighting patterns on main and dip beam for two different units – a standard headlamp, on the right, and a quartz halogen unit, left. The improvement with QH is dramatic and well worth investment.

Smaller machines are usually badly underlit with lights ranging from 35 to 25 watts on high beam. The alternators on these bikes are not very powerful – 100W or less – and normally they have batteries with a small capacity – 5 amp-hours is typical. Thus the electrical system does not leave much in reserve to power extra lighting, and it would not take long to run the battery flat.

One answer is to fit a more powerful bulb, up to say 40 or 45 watts on high beam. This may stretch the alternator, but the low beam will be less powerful around the 35 watt mark and within the machine's limits. Therefore, so long as high beam is not used continuously, the system will work. If main beam is used too much the battery will run down, causing the lights to dim as the engine slows down and possibly causing misfiring. The only way out then is to run on low beam to get some charge back into the battery. A longer period of use can be had by fitting a larger battery, simply because a 10 amp-hour battery takes twice as long to run down as a 5 amp-hour one, supplying the same current. The battery, however, will be physically larger too, so check that you have room to fit it – Japanese machines in particular tend to have everything squeezed into the smallest possible space.

To find out whether your electrical system can take the changes you propose to make, there is an easy way of working out how close to the limit you are getting. You need to know the alternator's rated output and the capacity of the battery which are usually quoted in the manufacturer's handbook. Then you add up the loads which will be used in the electrical system (in watts, the wattage rating is the current taken multiplied by the voltage; i.e. amps x volts). These will include the head-light, tail-light, instrument lights, ignition, and for short periods the stop-light and direction indicators.

Fitting quartz halogen units can pose problems too, as many of them are rated at 50 to 60 watts. The biggest snags, however, are usually physical rather than electrical. Quartz halogen units usually have a greater depth than standard lights, and are sometimes difficult to fit into the headlamp shell. It may be necessary to cut and reshape the shell or to fit an alternative one.

Early quartz halogen lights were fragile and did not stand up too well to motorcycle vibrations. Later ones are a lot better, however, with twin bulb types being even more robust than the dual-filament type.

Basic maintenance

On some machines it is possible to improve the lighting, but on many the lights are powerful enough, except that the power never gets through to them. The biggest dissipators of power are switch contacts, which get dirty and corroded, and earth connections. It is fairly easy to scrape the switch contacts clean and to make sure they mate firmly together and to clean up the snap-connectors. It is also worth taking an additional earth lead from the headlamp to a good contact like the engine mounting bolts and to check the wiring for chafing, which could break some of the metal strands even if the outer insulation is not torn.

Even when the power has an uninterrupted journey to and from the lamp, the light beam still depends upon it being clean, and the internal reflector also being clean. The internal reflector, particularly those on quartz halogen units, should not be touched even by clean fingers. There is apparently no known way of cleaning them. For what amounts to just not keeping things clean, you could lose easily 10 percent of the electrical input and another 10 percent of the light output.

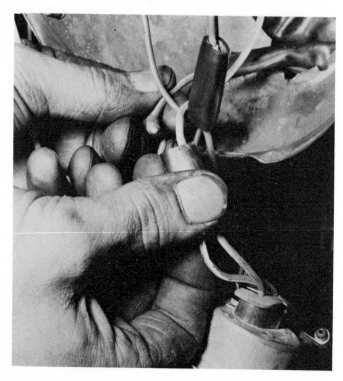

Wiring connections can absorb power if they are dirty or loose, reducing brilliance.

If the battery keeps going flat it may be due to the charging system. There is no easy way to boost the charging system. Although it may be possible to fit a more powerful alternator, if the electrical equipment is all standard there should not be any need for more power. So, before considering improving the charging system, the first thing to do is discover why the battery runs down.

If too many or too powerful lights are used, one answer is either to use them less, or to fit a larger battery. This will not solve the problem – it will just slow it down. Fitting a more powerful alternator is the only real solution.

Fault finding

A voltmeter, ammeter, ohm-meter and a hydrometer are not essential but only by using these instruments will you achieve a definite idea of what is happening. For example, by the time the lights go dim the battery will be almost flat, whereas an ammeter would have told you it was discharging from the start.

If the battery is in good condition and is getting a charge from the alternator – i.e. the ammeter does not show a discharge or the voltage is kept above 11.5 or 5.5, depending upon the system – then any fault lies in the light circuit itself and will probably be a dirty switch contact or a poor earth [ground] connection.

All that can be done to maintain the battery is to keep it topped up with distilled water and make sure the connections are clean. Any internal fault almost certainly means a new battery.

A permanent discharge means that the system is using more power than the alternator can supply. The fault could be that the lights are too big or that a partial short circuit is draining the current away. Otherwise it means the alternator is not doing its job or a faulty rectifier is stopping the power getting through.

Many alternators are not connected for full output until the lights are switched on, and this involves additional connections from the alternator to the light switch. A faulty contact here will rob the system of power when it needs it most.

The last alternative is a fault in either the alternator or regulator. This can be tested for in the manner described on page 75.

Converting an alternator

Alternators tend to produce greater voltages according to how fast they are turned. But you will not be able to get any more electrical power from it, so its wattage rating will stay the same or possibly be reduced. To find out whether it is possible in practice to run a 6V system at 12 volts you will need to measure the open circuit voltage produced by the alternator. Disconnect the battery and run a separate lead from it to the ignition coils, so the engine can be run but without the alternator charging the battery. If the alternator is only connected for full output when the headlight is on, switch on the lights after removing the bulbs. Connect a voltmeter, reading at least up to 20V, across the DC terminals of the rectifier and run the engine at normal speeds. The reading is the no-load voltage and obviously has to be over 12V, and should be over 15V, otherwise the conversion cannot work, as the alternator needs to supply this much under full load.

Calculations for changing an alternator

If the alternator's output at 6V is quoted as 100W, this means it can supply a current of 100/6 amps. If the no-load voltage measured is 18V, it means that the resistance of the coils is 12 x 6/100 ohms (voltage divided by current). This resistance is the same all the time – so to tap 12 volts from the alternator, the maximum current available will be the open circuit voltage less the new nominal voltage (18-12), divided by the resistance (72/100), which gives 600/72 amps. This, multiplied by 12 (the new running voltage) to give the power of the alternator, brings us back to 100W, so in this example the conversion would be quite feasible.

Going through the same process but using a no-load voltage of 15, gives a figure of only 66.7W – so the conversion is not viable. To make a 12V conversion all 6V components must be replaced with their 12V equivalents, all connected in the same way as the original parts. If the alternator is re-wired for full output a Zener diode and a suitable heat-sink should also be used.

Direct lighting and indicators

It is possible to fit indicators to a direct lighting system but the bike will have to be re-wired so that the generator output is fed to a rectifier instead of the lights. The rectified current can then be used to charge a battery and this will supply the rest of the electrics. The only real use on small machines would be to maintain reasonable light power at idle and to act as a stabilizer for indicator circuits, but because these generators, particularly on mopeds, are generally so feeble, there would be very little benefit in return for a lot of work.

Fitting indicators to these types of machines is hardly worthwhile. To adapt the wiring to take a battery is difficult and costly, while the results would still be doubtful. Other kinds of indicator kit with independent batteries, work, but the batteries have to be replaced frequently if the indicators are used in a normal manner. A point to consider is the legal aspect; for if fitted, the indicators must work and a flat battery is no excuse. They also have to flash at between 60 and 120 times per minute, which with any fluctuating voltage source could be difficult to guarantee.

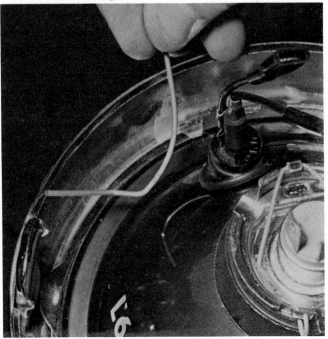

Fitting a light unit to a headlamp rim using W clips. Poor fittings may damage the unit.

Electrical fault finding

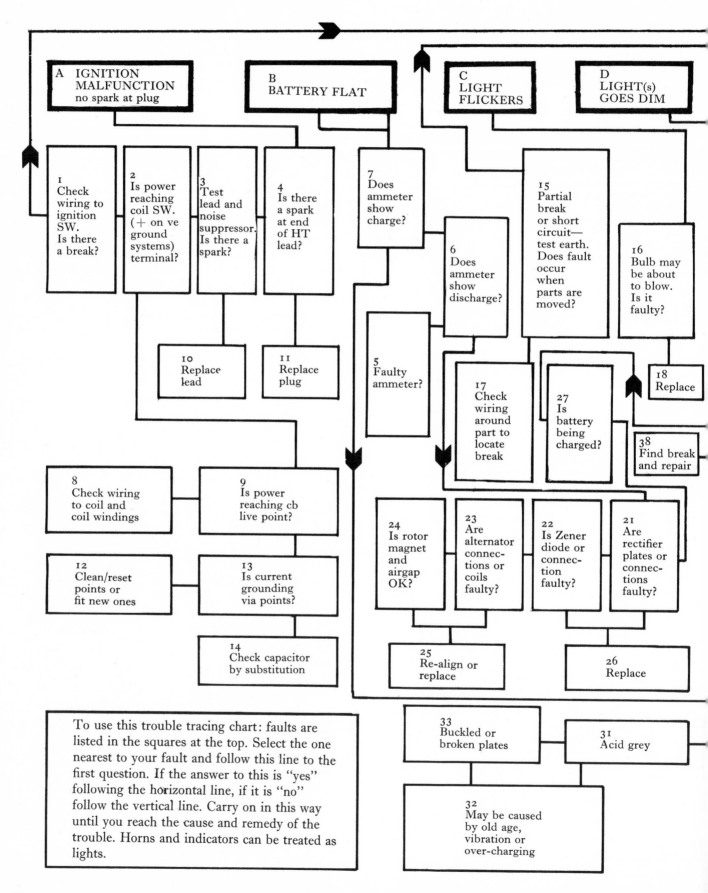

A IGNITION MALFUNCTION no spark at plug

B BATTERY FLAT

C LIGHT FLICKERS

D LIGHT(s) GOES DIM

1 Check wiring to ignition SW. Is there a break?

2 Is power reaching coil SW. (+ on ve ground systems) terminal?

3 Test lead and noise suppressor. Is there a spark?

4 Is there a spark at end of HT lead?

7 Does ammeter show charge?

15 Partial break or short circuit— test earth. Does fault occur when parts are moved?

16 Bulb may be about to blow. Is it faulty?

10 Replace lead

11 Replace plug

6 Does ammeter show discharge?

5 Faulty ammeter?

17 Check wiring around part to locate break

27 Is battery being charged?

18 Replace

38 Find break and repair

8 Check wiring to coil and coil windings

9 Is power reaching cb live point?

12 Clean/reset points or fit new ones

13 Is current grounding via points?

24 Is rotor magnet and airgap OK?

23 Are alternator connections or coils faulty?

22 Is Zener diode or connection faulty?

21 Are rectifier plates or connections faulty?

14 Check capacitor by substitution

25 Re-align or replace

26 Replace

To use this trouble tracing chart: faults are listed in the squares at the top. Select the one nearest to your fault and follow this line to the first question. If the answer to this is "yes" following the horizontal line, if it is "no" follow the vertical line. Carry on in this way until you reach the cause and remedy of the trouble. Horns and indicators can be treated as lights.

33 Buckled or broken plates

31 Acid grey

32 May be caused by old age, vibration or over-charging

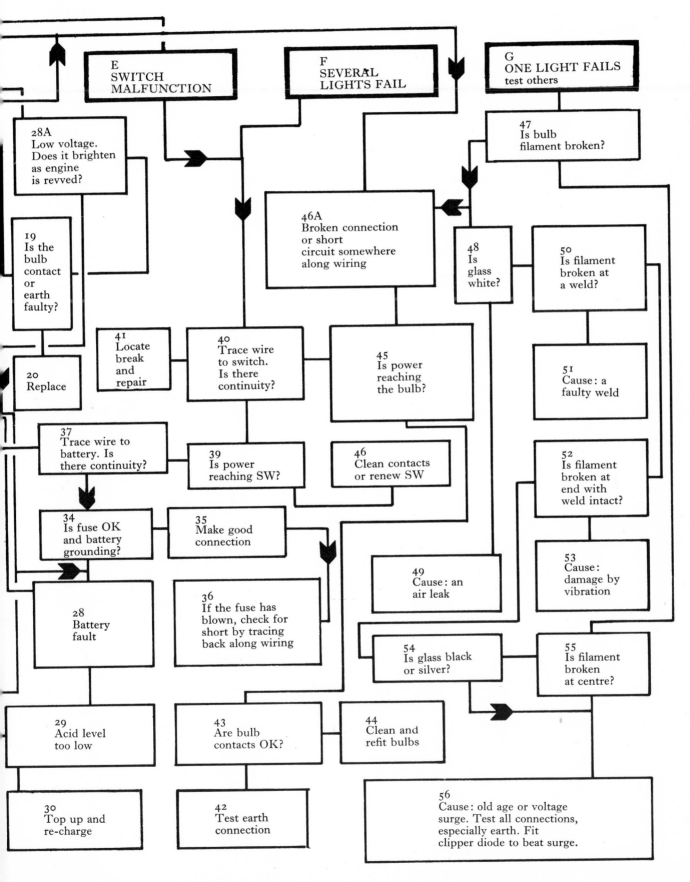

E
SWITCH
MALFUNCTION

F
SEVERAL
LIGHTS FAIL

G
ONE LIGHT FAILS
test others

28A
Low voltage.
Does it brighten
as engine
is revved?

47
Is bulb
filament broken?

19
Is the
bulb
contact
or
earth
faulty?

46A
Broken connection
or short
circuit somewhere
along wiring

48
Is
glass
white?

50
Is filament
broken at
a weld?

41
Locate
break
and
repair

40
Trace wire
to switch.
Is there
continuity?

45
Is power
reaching
the bulb?

51
Cause: a
faulty weld

20
Replace

37
Trace wire to
battery. Is
there continuity?

39
Is power
reaching SW?

46
Clean contacts
or renew SW

52
Is filament
broken at
end with
weld intact?

34
Is fuse OK
and battery
grounding?

35
Make good
connection

53
Cause:
damage by
vibration

49
Cause: an
air leak

28
Battery
fault

36
If the fuse has
blown, check for
short by tracing
back along wiring

54
Is glass black
or silver?

55
Is filament
broken
at centre?

29
Acid level
too low

43
Are bulb
contacts OK?

44
Clean and
refit bulbs

30
Top up and
re-charge

42
Test earth
connection

56
Cause: old age or voltage
surge. Test all connections,
especially earth. Fit
clipper diode to beat surge.

Glossary

Accelerator pump – a plunger fitted to some carburettors, operated by the throttle cable, which forces extra fuel into the airstream as the throttle is opened. The faster it is opened, the greater the pumping effect. The intention is to richen the mixture temporarily to give quicker response and optimum power for acceleration.

Advance – of ignition and valve timing, the distance before top dead centre (TDC) or bottom dead centre (BDC) that the spark fires or the valve opens. May be measured either directly from the piston, eg 3.2mm (⅛in) before TDC means 3.2mm (⅛in) before the piston reaches the top of its stroke. Or it may be measured in degree of engine rotation, eg 15° BTDC means that the engine would have to turn another 15° before the piston reached the top of its stroke. An advance curve is a method of showing the increasing amounts of advance that an engine needs as it goes faster. The reason that advance is needed at all is because things like combustion take time to happen; the design of the ports and head, the compression ratio and the engine speed all have an effect on this. The nett result is that if the spark is fired a certain time before the piston reaches the top of the stroke then by the time the combustion is under way and is starting to exert a pressure on the piston, it will have reached the top and the expanding gas can push it down a full stroke.

AF – across-flats, measurement on square or hexagonal parts, usually nuts and bolts, between opposite sides. Used to denote spanner sizes as an alternative to quoting the thread size which they fit.

Air lever – a control to alter the mixture strength manually on some carburettors. May be in the form of a choke, which simply restricts the airflow through the carburettor for starting or may be designed for general running adjustments, as on the Amal TT carburettor.

Air jet – plug with a small orifice, which can be changed for one of greater or smaller size, fitted into the air passage leading to the pilot jet in some carburettors. This allows some adjustment of the airflow and can be used to adjust the idling mixture.

Air slide – air valve or throttle. In a carburettor, a valve which opens and closes the main air passage. It is usually connected directly to the twistgrip and also operates a needle valve which

regulates the petrol flow at the same time. In some carburettors (constant velocity types) the air slide is lifted by the engine vacuum produced in the intake and closes under its own weight or by a small spring.

Alternating current – an electric current which reverses its direction or polarity in a cyclic manner, ie it continues to reverse direction regularly.

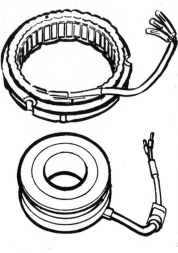

Alternator

Alternator – generator which produces alternating current. It consists basically of a magnet which is rotated (by the engine) and a number of coils are mounted around the magnet. The effect of the moving magnetic field is to generate a current in each coil as the magnet passes it. The direction of the current depends upon the movement of the magnet (always in the same direction) and the polarity of the magnet. Thus as the North pole passes each coil a current is generated in one direction, then as the south pole passes the same coil, the direction is reversed. A variation on this theme is to have the magnet (rotor) fixed and the coils (stator) fixed, while a shaped ring fitted between the two is turned by the engine. This deflects the magnetic field and produces the same effect.

Instead of using a permanent magnet, some alternators have an electro-magnet or field coil. This is energised from the battery via brushes and slip rings and this type is called separately excited. It has the advantage of greater output on full load and the ability to control the output by varying the current through the field coil.

Ammeter – an instrument which measures electrical current (in amps). Usually the current is passed through a small coil, producing a magnetic field in proportion to its size. A bar magnet is pivoted in this field, held by a light spring, so that it is deflected by the field produced by the current. The needle is connected to the bar magnet.

Armature – the central spindle or shaft of an electrical generator or motor which carries the windings of the coils, etc.

Aspect ratio – the ratio of height to width, usually quoted for tyres. A figure of .8 or 80 per cent would mean 127mm (5in) width for a 102mm (4in) height.

ATD – automatic timing device, which controls the advance of an engine's contact breaker. The breaker cam is mounted on a plate carried on two hinged arms. The faster the shaft turns, the greater the centrifugal force on these arms and the more they open outwards. In doing so they turn the cam, causing it to operate the contact breaker sooner, advancing the ignition timing. As the engine slows down, springs return the arms, and the cam, to their normal position. The springs can be varied to give different characteristics.

BA – British Association. A fine thread form on small diameter screws and bolts, used for electrical components etc.

Baffle – a plate or other obstruction in a passageway arranged so that any fluid flowing through the passage has to go around it. Used to deflect exhaust gases as a means of silencing, or to collect drops of oil to drain them back into the sump.

Balance shaft – an alternative method of balancing pistons is to have part of the weight balanced at the crankshaft and the rest balanced on one or two separate shafts, arranged to turn so that they balance out at mid-stroke positions as well as at BDC and TDC.

Ball valve – a one-way valve made up of a ball bearing sitting on a conical seat. Fluid flows up through the centre of the conical seat, easily lifting the ball. The weight of the ball, sometimes aided with a spring, prevents the fluid going back as the fluid tends to push the valve closed. Used mainly to prevent oil draining back along a pipe, also with adjustable spring tension as a pressure relief valve – the

spring holds the ball on the seat until the fluid on the other side has built up enough pressure to overcome the spring. Worn seats can be reformed by holding a drift against the ball and giving it a sharp tap.

Banjo union – a method of connecting pipes carrying oil or petrol [gas] to passageways cast into the engine. The pipe has a circular fitting at its end, through which a hollow bolt fits. The liquid enters the bolt through holes drilled in the stem and goes through the centre of the bolt which is screwed into the engine casting etc. Used on rocker feeds, carburettors etc.

Battery – series of electrical cells which when charged store electrical power. The power is available by an electro-chemical process between the metal (lead) plates and the electrolyte (dilute sulphuric acid). In a fully charged condition the electrolyte has a specific gravity of 1.260 or more if the temperature is below 80°F. Fully discharged the SG will fall to 1.122 or less if the temperature is above 40°F.

Battery

BDC – bottom dead centre. The lowest point reached by the piston (or the point farthest from the cylinder head). In this position the centres of the big end, crankshaft and small end will be in line.

Bearing – any part or surface which supports another part is a bearing although the meaning is usually restricted to parts which are moving relative to one another. Sometimes the bearing surface is formed on the parts themselves but where high loading or high speeds are involved another material is placed between the two and usually a film of oil is pumped in to avoid 'solid' friction. There are nume-

Bearing

rous types of bearing ranging from the plain bush to multiple row taper rollers.

Roller bearings are usually an interference fit in the housing which carries them and on the shaft which they carry and may need heat or a press to remove them. Others are located by circlips or dowels.

Shell bearings should always be tightened down to the correct torque and, in the case of big-end and main bearings, new bolts fitted as the old ones will have stretched and may have fatigued. The end caps must also be fitted the right way round on the journal they were originally fitted to because they are line bored and there will be small differences which would prevent the wrong one tightening squarely on to the bearing, causing it to tighten up and possibly prevent the shaft from being turned.

Scoring or signs of picking up on shell bearings, or if the journal is more than .001 inch out of round, mean that the journal will have to be reground and new undersize shells fitted.

On roller bearings any detectable radial play is too much. A worn bearing will sound noisy when it is spun and may even rattle when it is shaken.

Bleed – a vent removing excess gas or liquid, or a pressure take-off. To remove air from the fluid in an hydraulic system.

Bleed nipple – a small valve in an hydraulic line. When opened it allows the fluid to be pumped out so that contaminated fluid or air bubbles can be removed.

Blow-by – during combustion, the expanding gases escaping past the piston because of bore wear or a piston ring failure. As well as reducing engine efficiency this pressurises the crankcase and can cause high oil consumption.

Blowdown – the exhaust phase, particularly on a two-stroke where the burnt gases discharge under their own pressure.

Boost port – an additional transfer port in a two-stroke with a slightly longer open period than the main ports. On some motors it is simply a pocket machined in the cylinder in which a small amount of compressed charge is trapped and then released at the optimum time to increase turbulence or scavenging.

Bore – the diameter of a cylinder. To machine the cylinder to the correct size.

Breather – a vent to atmosphere, particularly from an engine compartment which may be pressurised. Can be a plain pipe, have a one-way valve, or a timed disc valve. Breathers with valves are used to keep crankcase pressure below atmospheric, placing the minimum resistance under the piston and helping to keep the engine oil-tight.

Bridged port – the cylinder wall left intact down the centre of a port to prevent the piston rings spreading into the port and catching the edges as the piston travels past it.

Brush – an electrical pick-up to take power off a moving part. Usually made of carbon.

BSF – British Standard Fine.

BSW – British Standard Whitworth.

Bush – see Bearing.

By-pass filter – an oil filter with a release valve on its feed side,

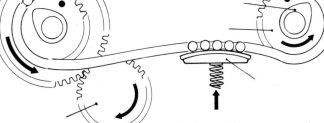

Chain tensioner arrangement

arranged so that if the filter becomes clogged or obstructs the oil flow the oil can by-pass it and so not reduce the supply to the engine.

Butterfly valve – a disc, pivoted across its centre, placed in a carburettor or intake tract as a throttling valve.

Cam – a part which when turned on its axis can give linear motion to another part (the cam follower) at 90° to this axis. May be in the form of an eccentric shaft (camshaft), a plate or a ring.

Cam follower – the part located on the operative part of the cam. The profiles of the cam surface and the follower determine the motion of the follower as the cam is turned.

Cantilever – a load-bearing or stressed member which is only supported at one end, like a diving board. Applied to swinging arms where the springs are not carried on the arm which carries the wheel.

Capacitor – an electrical component consisting of two conductors separated by a non-conductor (or dielectric). It acts like an electrical spring in that it can store a charge but only for a very limited time. The unit of capacitance is the Farad.

Carburettor – a device for accurately mixing air and fuel in the correct proportions for total combustion and for metering the fuel flow to the engine to govern its power and speed. Petrol [gas] is supplied at a constant head of pressure from the float bowl and is drawn into the venturi by the depression caused by the air moving through it. The air flow is regulated by a valve or throttle and the fuel flow by a series of jets, one of which is variable having a tapered needle also connected to the throttle, lowered into it.

CDI – capacitor discharge ignition. In a typical system, a dc-dc converter transforms the 12V battery voltage to 300V and charges a large capacitor. A small pulse from a magnetic pick-up or through contact breakers is used to trigger this, via a thyristor, causing the capacitor to discharge through the ignition coil to fire the spark plug.

Chain tensioner – a spring-loaded pulley or sprocket (jockey sprocket) or a plain-faced 'slipper' which bears on the slack or non-driving length of chain to take up slack. The tensioner may be adjusted by a spring, by oil pressure, or a manual threaded adjuster.

Circlip – spring clip formed into part of a circle, which fits into a groove to prevent a part from moving. May be an internal type, fitting inside a tube, or an external one, fitting around a shaft.

Clearance – the gap between two parts. May be a negative quantity, usually called a pre-load or an interference fit.

Clevis – a pivoted linkage joint made up from a shackle and a pin, usually located with split pins.

Clipper diode – a type of semi-conductor which only becomes conductive above a prescribed voltage. Connected in parallel with the lights, etc, it prevents voltage surges from damaging them.

Clutch – part of a transmission drive which can be engaged and disengaged manually or automatically. Motorcycle clutches usually have flat plates, alternately plain metal and coated with a friction lining. A chain or gear drives the clutch body which is engaged with one set of plates (the driving plates). These have tabs on their outer edges which locate in slots in the clutch body. The other set of the plates (the driven plates) are splined on to the clutch centre, which in turn drives the input shaft to the gear box. The two sets of plates are forced together by springs mounted on the pressure plate at the end of the clutch. The release mechanism forces this plate out reducing the spring pressure and allowing the plates to slip over one another.

Clutch drag – a malfunction in which the clutch will not free properly, caused by incorrect adjustment and the release mechanism not lifting the pressure plate evenly.

Clutch slip or spin – a malfunction in which the clutch will not transmit the drive. Caused by incorrect adjustment, weak springs, worn friction linings, buckled plates, oil on the plates, etc.

Coil – an electrical winding in the form of a loop or coil, in practice with hundreds or even thousands of turns. A current passing through a coil creates a magnetic field and a magnetic field can be used to create a current in the coil, which is the basis of generators. The magnetic field can also be used to move an iron plunger, as in solenoids, relays and voltage regulators. In ignition coils there are two windings, one which produces a magnetic field, which, when it collapses as the circuit is broken, induces a high voltage current in the second winding.

Collet – a circular, sometimes tapered, clip, often in two halves (split collet) used to hold a part to a shaft. Most common use is to clip into a groove on a valve to hold the spring collar to the valve.

Commutator – the end of an armature which is divided up into segments, electrically insulated from one another. Each opposite pair of segments are connected to a winding and brushes bear on opposite sides of the commutator to supply power to each winding in turn as the armature spins round. Used in DC motors and generators.

Compression ratio – the ratio between the volume above the piston at BDC and that at TDC. This is sometimes called the geometric ratio, while the corrected ratio as used by most Japanese manufacturers uses the volume above the piston at the point where the exhaust valve or port has just closed.

Connecting rod – the piece which joins the piston to the crankshaft. The bearing which carries the piston is called the small end while the one mounted on the crankpin is called the big end.

Constant mesh – in gearboxes, where all of the pinions are continually engaged with their partners. Gear selection is made by locking the appropriate pinion to its shaft or to the next pinion along the shaft by splines and dogs.

Contact breaker – an electrical switch, usually mechanically operated.

Cotter – a tapered pin, with threads at the narrow end. Tightening the nut pulls it tightly into the hole. Used to hold levers on to shafts.

Crankshaft – the shaft which is turned to provide the engine's motive force. The main bearings, which are supported in the crankcase are all in line and the crankpins are offset, thus as it turns the connecting rods and pistons are pushed up and down. The crankshaft may be made in one piece, or as several units which are either pressed or bolted together.

Cross-ply – tyre construction in which the strips of base material are set at an acute angle to the rim and cross one another.

CV – constant velocity. Type of carburettor in which the throttle is raised by engine vacuum with the intention of keeping the gas in the venturi at constant velocity at all engine speeds.

Cycle thread – a fine thread form.

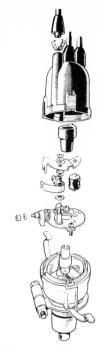

Distributor

Decompressor – a small valve usually operated by a cable and lever which opens a port in an engine's cylinder head, to facilitate starting or to stop the engine.

Damper (shock absorber) – device which slows down or inhibits the movement of a part, especially a sprung part or one which tends to oscillate.

Dashpot – a cylinder filled with oil used to damp the motion of a rod or piston moving up and down the cylinder. Found on some carburettors to prevent the airslide fluttering.

DC – direct current, electrical current which flows in one direction.

DC generator – a machine which produces direct current see Dynamo.

Desmodromic – type of valve operation which uses a cam (and rocker) to close the valve as well as to open it, doing away with the need for springs although light springs are often used to prevent chattering.

Diode – a device which will only allow electrical current to pass in one direction or under certain conditions. Originally from diode valve so called because it consisted of one anode and one cathode.

Direct lighting – an electrical system in which power for the lights and ancillary equipment is supplied direct from a generator, with no battery in the circuit.

Distributor – mechanical device to direct electrical current (usually high voltage current to the relevant spark plug). Only one low-tension circuit (contact breaker and coil) is used, the ht from the coil being supplied via a carbon brush to a rotor arm which is arranged so that it is passing one of several pole pieces at the right moment. The current arcs across to the pole piece and

then on to the plug.

DOHC – double overhead camshafts carried in the cylinder head, one to operate the intake valves and one to operate the exhaust valves.

Dry sump – engine lubricating system in which oil is pressure-fed to bearing surfaces, drains back to the bottom of the engine – usually the crankcase – and from there it is returned to a separate oil tank. This latter process is called scavenging and is performed by a pump of between two and five times the capacity of the feed pump to ensure that the crankcase is not allowed to fill up.

Dwell – of cams, the period in which the cam has no effect on the part it is operating (open dwell=full lift, closed dwell= fully closed).

Dynamo – a machine which produces direct current in much the same way as an alternator except the power is developed on windings carried on the armature and the reversing polarity is kept constant by connecting the windings to a commutator with brushes placed so that one is always positive and the other negative.

Dynamometer – a device for measuring power or rate of working. If work is equivalent to lifting a weight a certain distance, power is equivalent to lifting it this distance in a fixed amount of time. The dynamometer applies a load to the engine via some kind of brake, and the torque on this brake is measured. From this and the engine speed the horsepower can be calculated.

Earth – ground; a common connection for several electrical components.

Electronic ignition – solid state system in which a small

electric pulse (from contact breakers, magnetic pick-up, light cell, etc.) is amplified and used to trigger a circuit which controls the current flowing in the ignition coil.

Expansion chamber – an exhaust system contrived so that its shape will have a beneficial effect on engine power. This is based on the phenomena that gas flowing through a pipe will send back a high-pressure wave upon meeting a restriction or nozzle and send back a low-pressure wave if it is suddenly expanded or meets a diffuser. These waves travel at the speed of sound in the gas and the expanding and contracting shape of the chamber is arranged so that at a particular engine speed the pressure waves can help scavenge the cylinder as the exhaust opens and to push back 'lost' fresh mixture just before it closes.

Firing interval – the spacing in terms of crankshaft rotation between power strokes on a multi-cylinder engine.

Firing order – sequence of power strokes on a multicylinder engine.

Fixed jet – type of carburettor which has rigidly mounted fuel jets, volume flow being controlled by a movable air slide and a tapered needle moving inside one fuel jet.

Flame trap – baffle or wire gauze fitted to an engine's intake.

Flat engine – one with its cylinders set on opposite sides of the crankshaft (horizontally opposed).

Float – the free movement of a part on its own axis.

– carburettor component which floats in the petrol reservoir and closes a valve when the level reaches a determined height.

Float bowl – the petrol [gas] reservoir which feeds the carburettor with fuel at a constant head.

Float needle – a tapered valve which is pushed on to a conical seat by the float to shut off the supply of fuel.

Flywheel – a weight attached to the crankshaft whose inertia is sufficient to keep the engine turning between power strokes.

Four-stroke – an engine cycle which is made up of four phases; intake, compression, expansion and exhaust, each one taking a full stroke of the piston, and two turns of the crankshaft in all.

Fuel injection – pumping the required quantity of fuel into an engine where it mixes with the air in the cylinder or in a pre-mixing chamber. Two types have been used on petrol engines; the low pressure kind which pumps a continuous spray into the cylinder and the high pressure kind which injects a slug of fuel shortly before ignition.

Gallon – unit of volume equal to eight pints, 1605 cubic feet,

1205 US gallons, 4.55 litres. One gallon of water weighs 10 lb.

Gasket – a seal, usually soft or compressible, placed between two mating surfaces. Paper, cork and copper are commonly used.

Gas seals – any sealing mechanism which prevents gas escaping or a loss of pressure. May be designed like an oil seal, piston ring or labyrinth seal.

Gearbox

Gearbox – the housing containing gearwheels and shafts, or the complete assembly. In motorcycles two basic types are used; the traditional British type in which top gear is direct and the intermediate ratios are obtained by feeding the power from the mainshaft to a layshaft and back again; the other is the all-indirect or crossover gearbox in which power goes in on one shaft (input) and is taken off the other (output), involving only one pair of pinions per gear ratio.

Gear ratio – when two gear wheels of unequal diameter are meshed together they turn at different speeds. The ratio between the speeds is known as the gear ratio and is dependent upon the number of teeth on each wheel. Eg if the driving wheel has 20 teeth and the driven wheel has 40 teeth the ratio (40/20) is 2:1 and is called a reduction ratio because the driven wheel will turn at half the speed of the other. If an intermediate gear (an idler) is placed between the two, the ratio will not be changed, eg if an intermediate having 10 teeth were placed between the two in the above example it would turn twice for every revolution of the driving wheel, but it would only turn the driven wheel half a turn, maintaining the 2:1 reduction. Such gear trains are often arranged so that the number of teeth on the idler is not wholly divisible by the number of teeth on the other wheels, thus the same teeth do not mesh every time the wheels turn, evening out wear. This is called a hunting tooth arrangement. The pitch circle or diameter of the wheel is the effective diameter, ie: that which would give the same gear ratio if the two wheels had no teeth and relied upon pure rolling motion.

Gear selector – in gearboxes it is common to have mating gears on opposite shafts continually meshed (constant mesh). Some wheels are free to slide on their shafts but are forced to turn either by splines on the shaft or by dogs which mesh with another wheel on the same shaft. A particular gear is engaged by selector forks which push the pair of gears along the shafts until the dogs mesh with a wheel which is being turned by the engine. The selector forks are moved by a cam plate or cam drum which is turned by the lever via a pivoted quadrant. A sprung plunger holds the cam in position allowing the pedal to return to its normal position without moving the selector mechanism. This is called the positive-stop type of selector.

Generator – machine for producing electrical power. See Dynamo, Alternator.

Governor – device which limits or restricts the operation of another part. May be electrical, vacuum operated, mechanical, etc. A typical governor consists of weights attached to a shaft so that they move outward under centrifugal force as the shaft speeds up and this movement can be used to control the idling speed, advance or retard the ignition and so on.

Grommet – a soft plug used to block off a hole, often hollow to allow a cable to pass through, protecting it from chafing on the edges of the hole.

Ground – a common conductor used for several electrical devices. Earth.

Gudgeon pin (wrist pin) – a hardened pin which carries the piston, running in the small end bearing.

Hairpin spring – type of spring which, although it may have coils, depends upon the wire bending not twisting.

Horizontally opposed – engine configuration with the cylinders set on opposite sides of the crankshaft.

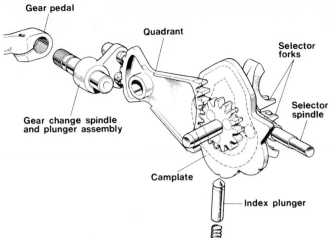

Gear selector mechanism

Horse-power – the unit for the rate of doing work, defined as 550 ft lb per second.

Hot spot – a point which gets unduly hot, possibly causing the fuel to ignite; or a point between intake and exhaust where the exhaust gases are used to warm up the fuel, making it more volatile.

HT – high tension.

Hub centre steering – arrangement in which the steering pivots are located inside the front hub.

Idler – gear placed between the input and output of a gear train. See Gears.

Ignition – any method of burning the fuel supplied to an engine. In petrol [gas] engines this is done by making an electric spark at the spark plug, by supplying it with a high voltage (10,000 to 30,000V). The source is usually either a coil or a magneto (see Magneto). A current from the battery flows through the primary winding of the coil and grounds via a set of contact breakers. At the point of ignition the contacts are opened by a cam and the primary current collapses, inducing a high voltage in a secondary winding which consists of many more turns, hence the increase in voltage. This is connected to the spark plug. A capacitor is connected across the contacts to prevent arcing caused by the self-induced current in the primary and to complete the circuit for the secondary current (both have a common ground on many systems). Alternative systems do away with the mechanical contact breaker by using a transducer (magnetic, infra-red light, etc.) which supplies a small pulse to trigger a transistorised circuit, causing a large capacitor to discharge through the primary coil winding.

Ignition advance – from the point of ignition to achieving full combustion takes a small but finite amount of time, depending on the pressure of the gas and the shape of the combustion chamber. In this time the piston will have moved a certain distance, and so in order that the full effect of expansion can hit the piston at top dead centre the ignition is started this distance before TDC. At higher engine speeds the piston will tend to move further and so the amount of advance has to be increased. See Advance.

Ignition timing – arranging for the contact breaker to open, or transducer to trigger, at the correct position in relation to the piston. May be done statically by setting the engine in the required position and then adjusting the contacts, or while the engine is running by connecting a stroboscope to the ht system and observing timing marks in its light. See Stroboscope.

Injector – type of fuel delivery in which the fuel is metered by a pump and forced into the air intake or the cylinder under pressure. The 'high pressure' type sends a timed slug of fuel into the engine while the 'low pressure' type has a continuous spray.

Intake – the part of an engine from the air cleaner to the valve or port through which air and fuel are drawn into the engine.

Journal – the bearing surface of a shaft, the part of a shaft supported by a bearing.

Leading shoe – the edge of a brake shoe facing the direction of rotation of the brake drum is known as the leading edge and because of the motion of the drum the force between shoe and drum will be greater here than at the trailing edge. A brake shoe which has its operating cam at the leading edge will therefore have more effect than one with the cam at the trailing edge as the force is increased by the drum's so-called servo effect. This arrangement is called a leading shoe.

Liner – an insert, usually cylindrical, pressed or shrunk into a component to provide a suitable bearing surface, to reclaim a worn component or to alter the size of the working surface. Cylinder liners which form part of the coolant jacket are called wet liners.

Long reach – spark plug which has a thread length of 19mm ($\frac{3}{4}$in).

Long stroke – engine in which the piston stroke is greater than the cylinder bore.

Low tension – low voltage, usually used to distinguish the 6 or 12V input to the ignition compared with its 10 to 30 kV output.

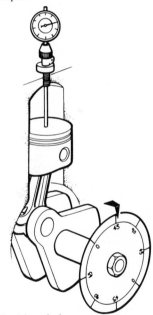

Ignition timing

Mag-dyno – magneto and dynamo as discrete units but mounted in a common housing and using the same drive.

Magneto – electrical generator with either fixed magnets or rotating magnets, primary and secondary windings and contact breaker points operated by the armature to interrupt the current generated in the primary. In the type which carry the coils on the armature the power to the spark plug is taken off from a slip ring.

Main bearing – bearing supporting the major shaft assembly – normally the crankshaft.

Main jet – orifice controlling fuel flow when the engine is run on full throttle. See Carburettor.

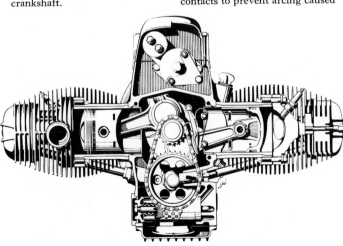

BMW horizontally opposed cylinders

Main shaft – major load bearing or power transmission shaft.

Manifold – pipe or tube with several branches eg to carry gas to or from the ports on a multi-cylinder engine.

Manometer – instrument for measuring pressure differences, consisting essentially of a U-tube containing liquid, pressure differences being shown by the liquid in one arm rising higher than in the other. .

Master cylinder – in a hydraulic system, the cylinder/piston assembly which is operated by the rider. The cylinder is filled with fluid from a reservoir and is smaller in diameter than the slave cylinders which actually operate the brakes, etc. The rider's force on the lever is transmitted to the piston and the pressure developed in the hydraulic line is proportional to this force divided by the area of the master cylinder. The same pressure is transmitted to the slave cylinders, which, having a greater piston area, receive a greater force, so the rider's effort is magnified.

Metre – unit of length = 39.37 inches.

Mixture strength – the air/fuel ratio, usually expressed in weights as the volume of a gas can easily be changed. The stoichimetric or chemically correct ratio to completely burn petrol is between 14 and 15:1 (air to petrol) while the ratio needed for maximum power is about 12:1 and that for maximum economy, consistent with even running, can be around 18:1.

Multiplate clutch – clutch with several plates, usually three or four driving plates and three or four driven ones, assembled alternately with the driving ones being connected to the clutch body via tabs on the plates and slots in the body while the driven plates are splined to the clutch centre. A pressure plate is fitted to the end which carries the thrust bearing for clutch release and the springs (usually coil springs) which force the plates together to engage the clutch.

Needle valve – a conical rod which is lifted or falls under its own weight, into an orifice to seal it, preventing fluid flow through the orifice. See Carburettor.

Octane – a rating of the anti-knock properties of a fuel, measured on a standard engine with a variable compression ratio. The higher the rating, the greater the anti-knock ability.

OHC – overhead camshaft. An engine in which the camshaft is carried in or above the cylinder head, operating the valves directly or via short rocker arms and doing away with the need for pushrods. The camshaft is driven at half engine speed by chain, shaft and bevel gears, toothed belt or gears.

OHV – overhead valve. An engine in which the valves are carried inside the cylinder head. The camshaft is usually located closer to the crankshaft (to simplify its drive) and the valves are actuated by a system of pushrods and rockers.

Ohm – unit of electrical resistance, that which takes a current of 1 amp when a potential of 1 volt is put across it.

Oil control ring – (scraper ring) a piston ring, often with slots cut in it, which is designed to remove excess oil from the cylinder walls. This prevents the oil from getting up into the combustion chamber where it would be burnt, causing high oil consumption and carbon fouling.

Oiled up – carbon fouling of a spark plug caused either by excess fuel or oil, or by using too hard a grade of plug, ie one which does not run hot enough to burn off deposits.

O-ring – a rubber or synthetic band fitted between two mating surfaces to give a seal. The ring is usually located in a groove.

Otto cycle – the sequence of events in an internal combustion engine, namely intake of fuel, compression, expansion and exhaust of the burnt fuel. These four distinct phases give rise to the four-stroke cycle, in which each one occurs over one stroke of the piston. Dr Otto was the first to describe this cycle.

Overhead cam – see OHC.

Overhead valve – see OHV.

Over-bore – to increase an engine's displacement by increasing the diameter of the cylinder.

Over-drive – a top gear which is too high to allow the engine to reach full speed. It allows cruising at lower engine rpm than with a 'correct' top gear, the idea being to save fuel and wear on the engine.

Over-geared – a machine on which the overall gearing, or top gear, is too high for it to reach full speed. Ideally the gearing should be arranged so that the engine can just reach maximum rpm in top gear – and that is the fastest it can possibly go. An over-geared machine will be slower because the engine will not have enough power to travel at the speed corresponding to peak rpm. An undergeared machine will also be slower because the engine will reach its rev limit at a lower road speed. In practice most roadsters are slightly over-geared as a safety factor, to prevent over-revving in top gear.

Pilot jet – small orifice or jet which controls fuel flow to the carburettor venturi when the throttle is closed ie it controls the mixture strength at tickover. See Carburettor.

Pinging – see Pinking.

Pinion – a gearwheel; the smallest of a pair of meshing gears.

Pinking [Pinging] – a knocking noise caused by incorrect combustion; likely to be traced to wrong ignition advance, overheating or fuel having too low an octane rating. The effects are a loss in power and possible damage to the piston crown.

Piston – a moving part which either compresses fluid in a cylinder or transmits the pressure force from the fluid.

Piston ring – a sealing ring, often of cast iron, which is an accurate fit in a groove in the piston. The ring may be of rectangular, tapered or L-section (Dykes ring) and is used either to give a pressure seal (compression ring) or to prevent too much oil working its way up the cylinder wall (oil control ring).

Piston ported – a description of a type of two-stroke engine in which the piston is used to open and close the ports. Alternatives include disc valves and reed valves.

Piston slap – a light rattling noise caused by wear between the cylinder and piston, usually heard first as the engine is taken off load.

Plug cap – a connector between the spark plug ht lead and the plug itself, usually with a shroud to protect the plug and incorporating a high resistance to suppress high frequency emissions which would cause interference on television and radio receivers.

Plug lead – heavily insulated cable carrying the ht current to the spark plug. May consist of metal or carbon strands.

Points – movable electrical contacts. See Contact Breaker.

Points gap – the gap between contact breaker points when they are opened to their maximum by the cam mechanism. This clearance determines how long (in terms of engine rotation) the points will be open and closed (points' dwell) which in turn governs the time allowed for the ignition coil to build up or discharge current.

Poppet valve – a mushroom-shaped valve which is supported on its spindle in a guide and uses the flat head to seal against a seat.

Power band – the range of engine speed in which useful power is produced.

Pre-ignition – ignition of the fuel in the cylinder before the spark occurs, caused by some malfunction such as carbon deposits glowing red-hot.

Primary drive – the drive (and reduction ratio) between the engine and clutch or gearbox. Chains, inverted-tooth chains, straight-cut gears and helical gears are the most common types.

Primary winding – in a transformer or induction coil, the coil carrying the initial current which is interrupted or varied to cause the required voltage across the secondary winding. This depends upon the ratio of the number of turns in the secondary and primary windings and on the rate at which the primary current is changed.

Push rod – a rod or tube used in compression to move a part such as a valve or rocker, or a clutch pressure plate.

Radial – along the axis of a radius. A radial ply tyre has the plies or strips of reinforcing material set at right angles to the edge of the tyre, whereas cross-ply tyres have them at a smaller angle, so that the plies cross one

Multiplate clutch set

another.

Rake – angled, usually to describe the angle of front forks or the steering axis from either the horizontal or vertical plane.

Ram effect – the self-compressing effect of a gas caused by its own momentum as it enters the cylinder of an engine. This conversion of kinetic energy into pressure energy allows the intake period to be extended into the compression stroke.

Reach – the length of a part, or the length of its fitting, eg the length of thread on a spark plug is known as the reach.

Rectifier – a device which only allows electrical current to flow in one direction (a semi-conductor or a valve) in order to produce direct current, eg for supplying a battery. A half wave rectifier is the simplest kind, admitting positive current while rejecting negative, so half of the ac input is 'lost' and not available on the dc output side. A full wave rectifier (bridge rectifier) forms an electrical one-way system which converts the full input into dc.

Rocker – a pivoted arm used mainly to transmit motion in valve gear. The pivot may be at the centre or the end of the arm.

Rocker box – housing or compartment which contains the rockers and adjustment for the valve gear, usually with an inspection window to provide access.

Rotary valve – valve formed by a disc or cylinder which is turned by the engine. Slots or ports are cut in it which line up with ports in the head, cylinder or crankcase to provide correct timing.

Rotor – a part which is turned eg the unit carrying permanent magnets or field coils in an alternator.

RPM – revolutions per minute.

Running in – a process of running in a machine gently when new to allow mating parts to bed in, avoiding scuffing and local heat build-up where parts are a tight fit.

Running on – a malfunction causing a motor to continue running after it has been switched off – usually because a hot spot in the combustion chamber is able to ignite the fuel.

Run-out – distortion in a shaft or wheel, measured as the total lateral displacement over one full turn.

Scavenge – to remove, usually applied to exhaust gases in an engine's cylinder or oil which drains into a 'dry' sump.

Secondary circuit winding – in a transformer or induction coil, the current and the circuit carrying it, produced by the fluctuations in the primary current.

Self-servo – using the action of a part to increase the force applied to it. For example the friction between brake drum and the leading edge of a brake shoe increases the pressure between

the two and increases the frictional force still further.

Servo – a mechanism to add power force to a manual control, often by connecting engine intake vacuum to a reservoir where the difference between this and atmospheric pressure acting on a diaphragm is used to supply additional force to assist controls.

Shaft drive – transmission which depends upon a shaft, usually driven by gears or bevel gears and incorporating a universal joint and a splined section to allow the shaft to follow suspension movement.

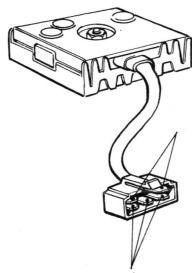

Rectifier with input and output points indicated

Shim – a piece of strip material used to pack out a part to adjust its position or the load on it.

Shock absorber – see Damper.

Short stroke – engine configuration in which the bore is greater than the stroke.

Single OHC – an engine with one overhead camshaft, operating both intake and exhaust valves.

Slave cylinder – a hydraulic cylinder in which pressure in the fluid moves a piston to actuate a part.

Sleeve – to fit a cylinder liner, either to restore a worn bore or to make the bore smaller.

Sleeve valve – a cylinder with port windows in it which is moved to align with ports for intake and exhaust.

Slick – a tyre with no tread pattern.

Slipper tensioner – a curved guide which sits along a run of a chain and is pushed against the chain to adjust its tension.

Sludge trap – an oil compartment to hold sludge deposits, often built into crankshafts where the more solid deposits are separated out by centrifugal force.

Small end – the connecting rod bearing which carries the gudgeon pin and piston.

Snail cam – a cam whose profile takes the form of a spiral, ie over one turn the lift steadily increases. Used to locate chain adjusters, etc.

Solenoid – an electrical coil, the magnetic properties of which can be used to move a small lever or

plunger. Used mainly in relays and electrical control systems.

Spark plug – device to introduce an electric arc inside the combustion chamber. The central electrode is connected to the ignition secondary circuit while the outer electrode is grounded and the gap between them adjusted to the maker's specification. The type of electrode and the characteristics of the ceramic insulator around it govern the temperature at which the plug runs. If it runs too cool for the engine it is fitted in it will not burn off fuel and oil deposits and the plug will foul,

eventually short-circuiting. If it runs too hot it will cause pre-ignition, running-on and piston damage.

Spark arrester – baffled chamber fitted to exhaust pipes of off-road machines to prevent burning exhaust gases causing forest fires.

Spline – regular grooves cut along a shaft to mate with similar shapes formed on a wheel so that the wheel may be locked to the shaft.

Split pin – a hairpin-shaped wire pin which may be pushed through a hole and the open ends splayed out to stop it falling out. Used to stop linkage joints drifting and to stop nuts coming undone.

Square engine – one in which the cylinder bore equals the stroke.

Stator – a static component such as the plate carrying the power coils on an alternator.

Steering damper – friction discs or a hydraulic damper which add resistance to the front forks moving from lock to lock.

Steering head – the bearings which connect the frame to the forks, determining the steering angle (castor) and the basic steering and suspension geometry.

Steering lock – the angle between the straight ahead and the full left or right turn positions. Also a small plunger or hook which can be used to lock the forks in the extreme position as an anti-theft device.

Steering stem – the spindle fixed to the bottom yoke of the forks which carries the bearings in the steering head.

Stroke – the linear displacement of a part such as a piston.

Sub-frame – an assembly fixed to the frame to carry eg the seat, suspension mountings etc.

Sump – a reservoir into which liquid, especially oil, can drain. On wet sump systems this doubles as the oil tank, on dry sump engines the reservoir is evacuated by a scavenge pump which returns the oil to the supply tank.

Supercharger – a compressor or pump driven by the engine which pressurises the air fed to the intake.

Suppressor – a high resistance, in the order of 10 kilo-ohms, in series with the spark plugs of an engine to cut down high frequency signals which produce noise on television and radio receivers.

Suspension – the sprung struts which support a vehicle and locate the wheels. These are pivoted to allow the wheels to follow the contours of bumps and to take up weight transfer under braking and acceleration, and are sprung to allow the suspension to return to its neutral position afterwards. The springing medium may be metal coil spring, torsion bars, rubber, or gas in compression and the action is usually damped

Rear suspension of a Yamaha XS/1100

hydraulically to stop the spring's tendency to continue bouncing.

Swing arm – type of rear suspension in which the wheel is carried in a fork or radius arm pivoted in front of the wheel, with spring and damper units mounted directly on the fork or on a linkage operated by the fork.

Taper roller – a bearing using tapered rollers set at an angle to the axis of the bearing so that it can take thrust as well as radial loads. See Bearing.

Tachometer – instrument for measuring engine rpm.

Tappet – a sliding block or cylinder which is supported to take side loads, set between the cam follower and the pushrod in OHV engines. On early machines the tappets were adjustable to provide valve clearance.

TDC – top dead centre; engine position when the crankshaft, big end and small end centres are all in line with the piston at its furthest from the crankshaft. This does not apply to engines which incorporate the Desone principle where one component is deliberately set a fraction out of line to reduce obliquity of the connecting rod, thus reducing amount of piston thrust on cylinder walls.

Telescopic forks – type of front suspension consisting of two tubes able to slide over one another on bushes with a spring in between. The compressive action is also used to effect damping by forcing oil through controlled apertures.

Tensioner – a device to take up slack in a chain, pulley, etc. May be a pulley, sprocket or slipper under spring or hydraulic pressure.

Thermal slot – a slot cut into a part which is subjected to high temperatures, eg a piston, to accommodate expansion and reduce the risk of distortion or seizing.

Thermostat – a temperature-controlled valve or switch. The most common motorcycle applications are on liquid-cooled engines where thermostats open a valve leading to the radiator when the engine reaches a certain temperature (80° to 90°C), or switch on a cooling fan when the coolant temperature reaches a certain level.

Three-phase – electrical system in which alternating current is generated in three coils arranged so that the three peak voltages are equally spaced (ie 120° apart). The coils are either star-connected (in the form of a Y with the three output leads taken from the ends of the Y) or delta-connected (in the form of a triangle with the output from each corner). Only three (instead of six) conductors are then required and at any one time the sum total of the voltage or the current is zero. If three-phase current is fed into three delta- or star-connected coils a rotating magnetic field is produced.

Throttle – a valve or restriction which reduces fluid flow in a tube. Used in carburettors to regulate the air flow and control the power produced by the engine.

Throttle cutaway – a wedge-shaped portion cut out of the throttle valve or airslide in a carburettor. The size of the cutaway determines the air flow at low throttle openings and can be changed to alter the carburation at these settings.

Throttle stop – a screw adjuster which can be used to alter the position of the airslide when the throttle is closed, to regulate the idle speed of the engine.

Thrust bearing, washer – a bearing designed to take axial as well as radial loads, a shim or washer which controls endfloat.

Timing – the point at which an operation (such as ignition or a valve opening) happens in relation to the position of the crankshaft when it happens. Usually measured from the TDC or BDC positions and expressed as degrees of crank rotation before or after TDC, or inches (or mm) of piston movement before or after TDC.

Timing light – a battery and lamp connected across the contact breakers to indicate when they are closed (light on) and open (light off).

Torque – a twisting force caused when a plain force does not act through the centre of a part and tends to make it turn. The amount of torque is the size of the force multiplied by the shortest distance from its line to the centre or pivot of the part. The units are lb-ft or kg-m.

Total loss lubrication – system in which metered quantities of oil are pumped into an engine with no scavenging or recirculation, the oil being burned or otherwise 'lost' immediately after it has passed the bearing surfaces.

Enduro bike two-stroke engine

Trailing shoe – a brake shoe operated at the trailing edge – see Leading shoe.

Transfer port – the passageway(s) in a two-stroke engine which deliver the fuel/air mixture to the cylinder from the crankcase.

Transformer – basically two induction coils with a different number of turns in them so that when alternating current is fed into one it induces ac at a different voltage in the other, eg in a battery charger where 240V AC is transformed to about 15V and then rectified to direct current to supply the battery.

Transmission – any means of taking power from the source to the part to be driven; may be gears, chain, belt, shaft, fluid or friction drive. See Gears.

Turbocharger – high-speed turbine driven by an engine's exhaust gases. It is geared to a similar compressor which delivers air to the intake. Versions can also be driven by belt and pulley rather than exhaust gases.

Two-leading shoe – a drum brake with two shoes, both operated at their leading edges to get the maximum self-servo effect from the motion of the drum. See Leading shoe.

Two-stroke – engine cycle which gives a power stroke at each revolution of the crankshaft (ie for every two strokes of the piston). As the piston rises it draws in fresh fuel and air to the crankcase, while compressing fuel from the previous cycle above it. This is ignited and the power stroke also compresses the mixture now in the crankcase. Just before BDC this mixture is pumped into the cylinder via transfer ports and at the same time the exhaust port is opened to allow the still-expanding burnt gases to leave the cylinder. Although there are twice as many power strokes compared to the four-stroke cycle, the two-stroke cannot produce twice as much power because the crankcase pumping losses are greater and the effective stroke is reduced by the opening of the exhaust port.

Vacuum gauge – a pressure gauge which records pressure below ambient or atmospheric pressure. Usually calibrated in inches of mercury (ins Hg) or of water, ie the pressure made by a column of this liquid so many inches high.

Valve bounce – most mechanically operated valves are returned by springs, which at some speed cannot keep up with the motion of the valve and allow it to float or bounce so that it doesn't close properly.

Valve cap – a hardened piece fitted over the end of a valve stem to protect it from the hammering of the operating gear. Also a sealed cap which screws on to the tyre valve to prevent pressure loss if the valve fails.

Valve collar – circular piece which fits over the end of valve springs, transmitting their pressure to the valve by being forced against a split collet located in a groove in the valve stem.

Valve lift – the distance a valve is lifted from its seat – often given as a maximum or at a certain crankshaft position as a method of timing the camshaft.

Valve lifter – a device to partially lift the exhaust valve, spoiling engine compression so that the motor may be turned over easily.

Valve seat – the sealing surface of the valve and of the housing with which it mates. To make a good seal the two are often

Two-leading shoe front brake

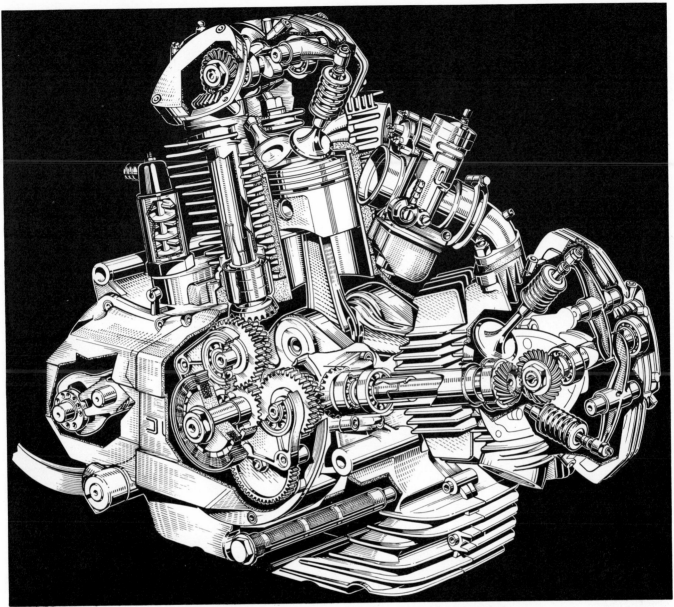

V-engine, examplified by one of the big Ducati motors

lapped together, turning the valve on the seat with an abrasive compound (grinding paste) between them.

V-engine – a piston engine with its cylinders set at an angle to one another and big-end bearings sharing the same crankpin for each pair of V-formed cylinders so that the angle of the V determines the firing period between each cylinder.

Venturi – a tube for fluid flow which is tapered to a smaller section and then expanded in order to increase the speed of the fluid at its narrowest point. As the pressure of the fluid decreases in proportion to its speed this is used to cause a pressure drop, for instance in carburettors.

Vertical twin – an engine with two parallel cylinders, normally set upright in the chassis with the crankshaft set across the chassis.

Viscosity – measure of a liquid's shear strength or resistance to flow. In practice it is measured by the time taken for a given quantity to flow through a standard orifice at a particular temperature and is quoted on the time scale for the test rig, eg Redwood scale, or given an arbitrary number rating, eg SAE numbers for lubricants. The SAE numbers increase for higher viscosity but different types of lubricant are not rated on the same scale, eg an SAE 80 gear oil has roughly the same viscosity as an SAE 30 engine oil. As the temperature of an oil increases its viscosity falls (it becomes runnier or thinner), which is why multigrade oils have additives such as VI modifiers, to reduce the change in viscosity at higher temperatures.

Volt – unit of electrical potential (force or pressure) which when applied across a resistance of 1 ohm produces a current of 1 amp.

Voltage regulator – device which regulates the electrical supply to the battery, increasing it as the battery voltage falls and decreasing it as the battery gets fully charged. On dynamos and separately excited alternators, battery power is used to supply the field coils and the regulator governs this supply, so controlling the output of the generator. When the battery is fully charged a larger current would be fed to the field coil, so a solenoid in the regulator is activated by this current and either breaks the field coil or switches in a resistance to cut down the current.

Wankel – type of engine with a rotary piston. The rotor, a triangular shape with curved sides, seals against an oval housing at its tips and is mounted eccentrically on the engine shaft. As it turns the volume between each rotor face and the housing increases and decreases and this is used to draw in gas through a port, compress it, ignite and expand it and let it blow down through another port.

Watt – unit of power, or rate of working, 746 watt being equal to 1 hp. In electrical units the power taken in watts is the product of the current and its potential (amps x volts).

Wet sump – lubricating system in which oil is carried in a reservoir or sump at the bottom of the crankcase. A pump supplies a pressure feed to bearings and the oil drains back into the sump with no scavenge or return pump.

Wheelbase – the distance between the centres or spindles of front and rear wheels.

Zener diode – a semi-conductor which is sensitive to voltage. The type used in motorcycle charging circuits is connected in parallel to the battery and as long as the battery voltage is below 13.5 to 14 volts the diode remains nonconductive. As the battery reaches this fully charged state the diode becomes conductive, absorbing the power from the generator and preventing overcharging.